Contents

Acknowledgements

The author and publisher are grateful to the following for permission to reproduce extracts and photographs:

Extracts 1.2, 1.8, 2.13, 2.16, 3.10, 4.5(a), 4.19, 4.25(a), 5.7, 5.13, 5.23, 5.26, 5.28, 6.9, 6.13(a), 6.15(a) Louis L. Snyder, ed., Documents of German History, copyright © 1958 by Rutgers, the State University. Reprinted by permission of Rutgers University Press; 1.7(a), 4.23, 5.2 J.C.G. Röhl, From Bismarck to Hitler, Longman Group Limited; 1.9, 3.21(b), 4.16, 5.9 A.J.P. Taylor, The Struggle for Mastery in Europe, 1848-1918, by permission of Oxford University Press; 1.10, 1.11, 4.13 V.R. Berghahn, Modern Germany, society, economy and politics, Cambridge University Press; 1.13, 2.3(b), 2.6, 2.12, 3.5 W.M. Simon, Germany in the Age of Bismarck, Routledge; 1.14 Fritz Stern Gold and Iron, reproduced by permission of Penguin Books Ltd./Alfred A. Knopf Inc.; 2.4 B. and M. Pawley, Rome and Canterbury through the Ages, Mowbray, an imprint of Cassell; 2.15(a), 2.15(b), 3.7, 3.8(b), 3.14(a), 3.19 L. Gall, Bismarck, the White Revolutionary, volume 2, Unwin Hyman Ltd.; 2.17(a), 3.21(a), 4.18 P.M. Kennedy, The Rise of Anglo-German Antagonism, 1860-1914, Routledge; 2.17(b), 4.20(a), 4.25(b), 6.19 H-U. Wehler, The German Empire, 1871-1918, Berg Publishers, Oxford/Washington, DC; 3.2, 3.4, 3.8(a), 3.8(c), 3.8(d), 3.12, 3.13, 3.15, 3.16, 3.17, 3.18 W.N. Medlicott and D.K. Coveney, Bismarck and Europe, Hodder Headline Plc.; 3.6 C. Grant Robertson, Bismarck, Constable Publishers; 3.9, A.J.P. Taylor, Bismarck, the Man and the Statesman, reproduced by permission of Hamish Hamilton Ltd.; 4.1(a), 4.1(b), 4.3, 4.4, 4.9, 4.10, 5.10 Lamar Cecil, Wilhelm II: Prince and Emperor, 1859-1900, copyright © 1989 by the University of North Carolina Press. Used by permission of the publisher; 4.2, 6.26 A. Palmer, The Kaiser, Warlord of the Second Reich, Weidenfeld and Nicolson Ltd.; 4.11, 5.3, 6.23(a), 6.23(b) I. Porter and I.D. Armour, Imperial Germany, 1890-1918, Longman Group Limited; 4.8, 4.14, 4.20(b) K.A. Lerman, The Chancellor as Courtier, Cambridge University Press; 4.15, 4.22, 4.24, 5.4, 5.15, 5.21, 5.24, 6.1, 6.3(a), 6.3(b), 6.12, 6.16, 6.17, 6.18 K.H. Jarausch, The Enigmatic Chancellor, Bethmann Hollweg and the Hubris of Imperial Germany, Yale University Press; 5.1, 5.5, 5.12(a), 5.12(b), 5.14, 5.16(a), 5.16(b), 5.19, 5.20, 5.22, 5.27 F. Fischer, War of Illusions, Chatto & Windus/W.W. Norton & Company, Inc.; 5.6, 5.11 N. Rich and M.H. Fisher, ed., The Holstein Papers, volume 1, Cambridge University Press; 5.8 D.C.B. Lieven, Russia and the Origins of the First World War, Macmillan Press Ltd.; 6.4, 6.7, 6.8, 6.24 R.B. Asprey, The German High Command at War, Little, Brown and Company; 6.5 C. Barnett, The Swordbearers, Eyre and Spottiswoode; 6.6, 6.10, 6.11, 6.13(b), 6.15(b), 6.22(a) F. Fischer, Germany's Aims in the First World War, Chatto & Windus/W.W. Norton & Company, Inc.; 6.14 R. Pipes, The Russian Revolution, HarperCollins Publishers Limited; 6.20, 6.21 F.L. Carsten, War Against War, British and German Radical Movements in the First World War, B.T. Batsford Ltd.; 4.6, 4.7 J.C.G. Röhl, Germany without Bismarck, B.T. Batsford Ltd.; 5.18 Friedrich von Bernhardi, Germany and the Next War, Hodder Headline Plc.

Photographs 1.1 Bismarck Museum/AKG, London; 2.5 Bildarchiv Preussischer Kulturbesitz; 4.5(b), 4.12 Punch Publications Ltd.; 4.21 Archiv der sozialen Demokratie der Friedrich-Ebert-Stiftung.

Every effort has been made to reach copyright holders. The publisher would be pleased to hear from anyone whose rights they have unwittingly infringed.

Introduction

The history of the Second Reich has inevitably been written in the shadow of the Third. In some cases this has been done quite deliberately. H-U. Wehler, in his influential book *The German Empire, 1871–1918*, first published in 1973 in its German edition, stated categorically: 'The guiding question underlying this book has been to investigate why Hitler's National Socialist regime came to power some dozen years after the monarchy ... The thread running through this book is the basic assumption that we cannot adequately grasp the history of the Third Reich without recourse to the history of the German Empire of 1871' (p. 7). Even those who dispute this thesis, such as Gerhard Ritter, have had to take his arguments into account, if only to expose what they take to be the discontinuities between Hitler's regime and that of Bismarck. But while this debate has dominated much recent historiography, an attempt has been made in this book to resist the temptation to look for parallels between the Second and Third Reich, or to establish causal connections between them. All roads surely do not lead to Hitler's assumption of power in 1933. The intention is rather to investigate the problem of why the German empire so proudly proclaimed in January 1871 came to such a humiliating end forty-seven years later.

Many explanations have been offered. Wehler argues that the empire was flawed from the start: 'As a result of three wars the Germans were given an Empire in the shape of a Greater Prussia which excluded Austria. It had been brought about by an extension of the "revolution from above" using military means.' It was the 'aristocratic forces of the military and the land-owners' who were the beneficiaries of this 'revolution from above' and it was these self-same groups who carried out 'an even more hazardous leap forward' that was to lead to the downfall of the empire in 1918 (Wehler, *The German Empire*, pp. 30–1).

Linked to this thesis is the argument associated with Fritz Fischer that, following the failure of the 1848 revolutions in Germany, the middle classes were effectively excluded from political power. The new German empire was thus dominated by entrenched elites drawn from the aristocracy, the civil service and the army. Rather than pursuing political goals, the German burghers found their fulfilment in a rapidly expanding industrial economy. The consequences, according to this view, have been summarised as follows: 'Never having undergone a bourgeois revolution as occurred earlier in England and France, Germany subsequently diverged further from the western democracies under the rule of Wilhelm. This divergence, or 'special path' (*Sonderweg*), not only explained the persistence of 'feudal elites' in German society, but it also illustrated the dangers of late industrialisation in a nation without the parliamentary traditions necessary to safeguard the diffusion of power. Social, economic and political tensions arising from rapid industrial change were incompletely deflected by ruling elites, resulting in an aggressive drive for world-wide influence (*Weltpolitik*) and territorial expansion. In short, Germany's unique misdevelopment in the nineteenth century explained her responsibility for twice unleashing war in the twentieth' (J. Retallack, 'Wilhelmine Germany', in Martel, *Modern Germany Reconsidered*, p. 37).

Such arguments have certainly drawn attention to the structural weaknesses of the empire, but do not take into account the influence of individuals or the play of events. A recent biographer of Bismarck quotes him as saying in 1881, in conscious reversal of Louis XIV's well-known remark 'L'État c'est moi', 'Moi, je suis l'État' (L. Gall, *Bismarck, the White Revolutionary*, vol. 2, p. 235). In Bismarck's case it was not an idle boast. The man who presided over the unification of Germany, and was chancellor for the first nineteen years of its existence played a dominating role in determining the course of the German empire, both at home and abroad. J. C. G. Röhl, citing Friedrich Naumann in 1900, credits Wilhelm II with a similar degree of influence: 'In present-day Germany there is no stronger force than the Kaiser ... No monarch of absolutist times ever had so much real power as the Kaiser has today ... ' (*Germany without Bismarck*, p. 279).

A recent biography of Bernhard von Bülow, chancellor from 1900 to 1909, concludes that his chancellorship 'was disastrous for Germany, and by any criteria represented nine mis-spent years' (K. A. Lerman, *The Chancellor as Courtier*, p. 258). It was Bethmann Hollweg, claims his biographer, who 'shaped the crucial decisions in peace and war' (K. H. Jarausch, *The Enigmatic Chancellor*, p. 400).

Nor should the impact of specific events be entirely discounted. Had there been no assassination attempts on Wilhelm I, Bismarck might well have failed to secure a majority in the Reichstag for his Anti-Socialist Law. Equally, without the successful assassination of Franz Ferdinand in 1914, those elements in Germany who were calling for a preventive war in 1912 might never have had the excuse they were looking for.

Thus the explanation for the failure of the Second Reich is to be sought in a complex blend of structural weaknesses, the failings and mistaken policies of individual politicians and untoward events. In the chapters which follow, an attempt has been made to give due weight to each of these ingredients.

The structure of the book keeps to the traditional chronological divisions: 1871, 1890 and 1914. It also maintains the distinction between domestic and foreign policy and this deserves a word of explanation. The validity of this distinction has properly been questioned. In the 1860s domestic considerations in Prussia, notably the budget, were subordinated to the requirements of foreign policy, especially the need for a large army.

Conversely, in the 1890s an adventurous foreign policy was seen as a means of resolving domestic tensions. Bülow, foreign secretary at the time, wrote in 1897: 'only a successful foreign policy can help to reconcile, pacify, rally, unite' (Röhl, *Germany without Bismarck*, p. 252). This interaction between foreign policy and domestic concerns is a marked feature of the German empire. During both Bismarck's and Bülow's chancellorships a policy of imperial expansion was adopted for largely domestic reasons. For the sake of clarity, separate chapters are devoted to foreign policy from 1871 to 1890 and from 1890 to 1914, but readers should be aware of the domestic context in which foreign policy decisions were taken and vice versa.

Within each chapter the attempt has been made to focus on the specific issues raised earlier, and to select documents relating to them. Thus Chapter 1 examines the nature of the empire, and the circumstances in which it came into being [1.1–1.4]; the effects of the treaty of Frankfurt and in particular the acquisition of Alsace-Lorraine [1.5–1.7]; the constitution of the empire as drafted by Bismarck [1.8]; and trends in the German economy and some of their social consequences [1.9–1.14].

Chapter 2 is concerned with Bismarck's rule at home and the controversies associated with it. How far was Bismarck a chancellor-dictator who prevented the emergence of a parliamentary system of government [2.1–2.3]? How did Bismarck treat those he deemed *Reichsfeinde* (enemies of the empire)? This question is examined first in the 'cultural struggle', *Kulturkampf*, he waged against Catholics [2.4–2.8] and then in his campaign against socialism and his efforts to take the wind out of its sails [2.9–2.15]. The chapter ends with Bismarck's decision to abandon free trade and to adopt a policy of protection in 1879, and the political consequences of that decision [2.16–2.17].

Bismarck's foreign policy is the subject of Chapter 3. Was it, as has sometimes been claimed, his main purpose to maintain harmony between the great powers, or were his motives less exalted [3.1–3.3]? This central issue is addressed by considering his policies in detail in relation to France [3.4–3.7]; the Near East [3.8–3.11]; the complex alliance system he painfully created [3.12–3.17]; and his brief flirtation with colonies [3.18–3.21].

The imperial regime at home after Bismarck's dismissal is the subject of Chapter 4. It begins with a study of the character and outlook of Wilhelm II [4.1–4.3]. There follows a brief account of each of Wilhelm's chancellors and his relationship with them [4.4–4.10]. The internal policy choices, and the party-political context in which they were made under the Wilhelmine regime [4.11, 4.12] are examined in relation to the following areas: tariffs and finance [4.13–4.15]; armaments and *Flottenpolitik* (the decision to build a large German navy) [4.16–4.20]; domestic reforms and the unsuccessful attempt to amend the Prussian electoral system [4.21–4.22]; and the government's response to anti-semitism and its handling of the Zabern affair [4.23–4.25].

Chapter 5 is devoted to German foreign policy from Bismarck's dismissal in 1890 until the outbreak of the First World War. It begins with an analysis of *Weltpolitik*, both as a concept [5.1–5.4] and as it was practised. Among its consequences were Germany's worsening relations with Russia, France and Britain and the emergence of the Triple Entente as a counterweight to the Triple Alliance. German responsibility for this outcome is examined [5.5–5.16]. Reference is then made to the worsening international climate and the growing demands for a preventive war between 1912 and 1914 [5.17–5.21]; the chapter ends with an examination of German policy in July 1914 and of the Fischer thesis that Germany not only risked war but actively encouraged it [5.22–5.29].

Chapter 6, on Germany and the First World War, concentrates first on German war strategy in the critical years 1917 and 1918, when German prospects of victory were at their best, and in particular on the decisions to adopt unrestricted U-boat warfare in January 1917 and to launch a great offensive on the western front in March 1918 [6.1–6.8]. It continues with a survey of German war aims both as a guide to German intentions and as a commentary on the failure to reach a compromise peace [6.9–6.15]. The final section deals with political developments during the war: the assumption of power by Hindenburg and Ludendorff; the growing polarisation of parties; and the final collapse of the empire [6.16–6.26].

In a book of this length many questions must remain unasked, let alone unanswered. It is hoped none the less that the documentary evidence presented will reveal something of the complexity and the paradoxes of the Second Reich. It was an empire which enjoyed universal suffrage (for the Reichstag) forty-seven years before Britain. By 1890 it had the most advanced social welfare system in Europe. The German Social Democratic Party was the largest single party in the Reichstag in 1912 at a time when the British Labour Party had barely got off the ground. Thanks to the industrial revolution, the rapidly increasing German population enjoyed rising living standards. Yet, as Bethmann Hollweg's biographer has put it: 'Incapable of reforming itself and not content with its share of the globe, Imperial Germany was not killed from the outside or revolution from the inside; it committed suicide' (Jarausch, *The Enigmatic Chancellor*, p. 404). How and why it did so is the central problem addressed in the following pages.

1 The creation of the German empire

The empire and the Franco-Prussian war

The Second German Empire owed its birth, if not its conception, to the Franco-Prussian War. This war, if not deliberately engineered by Bismarck, had at the very least been carefully prepared for. Bismarck had signed defensive treaties with the rulers of Baden, Bavaria and Württemberg in 1866 and, following the French declaration of war on Prussia on 19 July 1870, their armies came immediately to Prussia's assistance. By the beginning of August, 1.83 million German troops had been mobilised, of whom 460, 000 were poised on France's western frontier. On 1 September a French army surrendered at Sedan. On 3 September Napoleon was captured and on 4 September a republic was proclaimed in Paris. On 27 October the fortress of Metz capitulated. The bombardment of Paris began on 8 January 1871.

The scale and rapidity of the Prussian victory had two immediate consequences. As early as September 1870, in the wake of Sedan, Bismarck made clear his intention to annex Alsace-Lorraine. Once France had been defeated there was nothing to prevent the accession of the south German states of Bavaria, Baden and Württemberg to the North German Confederation, created by Bismarck in 1867, and the mood of nationalist euphoria evoked by victory overcame most, if not all, reservations there might have been among south German Catholics.

The empire was proclaimed in the Hall of Mirrors at Versailles on 18 January 1871 [1.1, 1.2], while the Franco-Prussian War was still smouldering. Armistice talks began under Bismarck's direction on 25 January, and preliminary peace terms were agreed on 26 February. They were finally embodied in the Treaty of Frankfurt, signed by the French and German governments on 10 May. At the same time a new constitution was adopted for the new empire and the terms of the treaty were defended by Bismarck at one of the first meetings of the new Reichstag. Thus the founding of the empire was irrevocably associated, both in German and French consciousness, with a militaristic triumph for Germany and a humiliating defeat for France.

The terms of the Treaty of Frankfurt were harsh. France was to cede Alsace-Lorraine to Germany in perpetuity; she was to pay an indemnity of 5 billion francs, and was to submit to a German army of occupation until such time as the debt had been met. The justice, or injustice, of these terms has been much debated. Bismarck defended them at the time on the grounds that France had been the aggressor and Germany needed protection [1.4]. His memoirs, written between 1890 and 1891, but not published until 1898, told a slightly different story [1.5]. Bismarck's German contemporaries seem on the whole to have approved wholeheartedly [1.6]. It is noteworthy, perhaps, that Bismarck's Jewish banker, Gerson Bleichröder, played a significant role in organising the financial mechanisms through which the indemnity was to be paid, though he did feel the amount was excessive. Opposition to the war and to the acquisition of Alsace-Lorraine was confined to a few liberal democrats and socialists [1.7].

The empire proclaimed with such a sense of triumph on 18 January was none the less a curious entity [1.3]. To the North German Confederation were now added the three south German states of Bavaria, Baden and Württemberg. But the frontiers of the new Germany did not accord very well with the nationalist spirit which had inspired its unification. The new empire now contained significant minorities which would never see themselves as German: Poles in the eastern provinces of Prussia, Danes in Schleswig and Frenchmen in Alsace-Lorraine. By 1910 they amounted to 4 million, out of a total population of 65 million. Conversely, there were substantial German minorities in the Habsburg empire, chiefly in Austria and Bohemia. While Wilhelm I, king of Prussia and the new emperor, might be recognised as the successor to Charlemagne, Franz Josef in Vienna had an equally strong claim to that title. The problem that had bedevilled the process of German unification in the first half of the nineteenth century, whether to adopt a *klein* (small) *deutsch* or a *gross* (large) *deutsch* solution, was not finally resolved in 1871. The *kleines Deutschland* that emerged was essentially an extension of Prussia, and very different, as it transpired, from the Germany envisaged by liberal politicians in 1848.

1.1   *The Proclamation of the German Empire*, by Anton von Werner, 1885

This celebrated picture, commissioned in 1871 to commemorate the proclamation of the German empire at Versailles, is here reproduced in its third version which was ordered to celebrate Bismarck's seventieth birthday in 1885. The artist, Anton von Werner, was present at the original occasion, which he remembered as short and drab. His first rendering of it was criticised for its emptiness, and the inconspicuous place given to Bismarck. In the second and third versions Bismarck was moved to the centre, dressed in the white uniform of the Cuirassiers and joined by the war minister, Roon (seen here on Bismarck's left), who had not been present on the actual day.

1.2   The imperial proclamation, 18 January 1871

Whereas, The German Princes and the Free Cities have called unanimously upon us to revive and assume, with the restoration of the German Empire, the German imperial office, which has not been occupied for more than sixty years; and Whereas, Adequate arrangements have been made for this purpose in the Constitution of the German Confederation;

    Therefore, we, Wilhelm, by grace of God, King of Prussia, do hereby proclaim that we have considered it to be a duty to our common Fatherland to respond to

5

the summons of the unified German Princes and cities and to accept the German imperial title. As a result, we and those who succeed us on the throne of Prussia, henceforth, shall bear the imperial title in all our relations and in all the activities 10 of the German Empire, and we trust to God that the German nation will be granted the ability to construct a propitious future for the Fatherland under the symbol of its ancient glory.

We assume the imperial title, aware of the duty of protecting, with German loyalty, the rights of the Empire and of its members, of maintaining the peace, 15 and of protecting the independent rulers of Germany, which, in turn, is dependent upon the united power of the people.

We assume the title in the hope that the German people will be granted the ability to enjoy the fruits of its zealous and self-sacrificing wars in eternal peace, inside boundaries that give the Fatherland a security against renewed French 20 aggression which has been lost for centuries. May God grant that we and our successors on the imperial throne may at all times enhance the wealth of the German Empire, not through military conquests, but by the blessings and the gifts of peace, within the realm of national prosperity, freedom and morality.

L. L. Snyder, *Documents of German History*, pp. 222–3

Questions

1 What is the significance of the choice of Versailles for the proclamation of the German empire [1.1]?

2 What can be learned from the changes made to 1.1 about how Bismarck's role in the creation of the German empire was perceived?

3 What was 'the German imperial office, which has not been occupied for more than sixty years' [1.2, lines 2–3] and why did Wilhelm I feel justified in assuming it?

4 Explain, and comment on, 'the fruits of its zealous and self-sacrificing wars' [1.2, line 19].

1.3 The German Reich in 1871

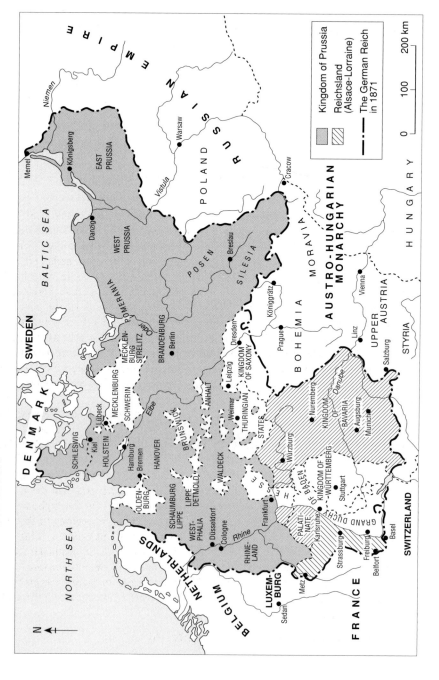

Questions

1 How far does the map [1.3] bear out the view that the German empire was 'essentially an extension of Prussia'?
2 Identify on the map [1.3] those areas inside the German Reich that were not mainly German-speaking and those areas outside it that were.
3 How much of a threat did Alsace-Lorraine pose to the security of Germany's western frontier?

1.4 Bismarck defends the acquisition of Alsace-Lorraine in a speech to the Reichstag, 2 May 1871

I remain convinced that the Germans were united in their desire for peace. But they were just as united when war was imposed upon us, when we were forced to take up arms for our defence. If God were to grant us victory in this war which we were resolved to wage bravely, then we were equally united in seeking securities which would make a repetition of such a war less probable, and should   5
it still occur, would make defence easier. Everyone remembered that there had scarcely been a generation of our forefathers not compelled to draw the sword against France and everyone thought that when Germany shared in victories against France opportunities had been missed to give us better protection against the West. This was because those victories were shared with allies whose interests   10
were not ours. So now that we had won a victory on our own, supported only by our own swords and the justice of our cause, we all resolved to work whole-heartedly to guarantee a secure future for our children.

In the course of centuries the wars with France had almost always resulted to our disadvantage as a consequence of German disunity. This had created a   15
geographical and military frontier which was for France always a temptation, for Germany always a threat.

The corner of Alsace around Weissenberg which forms a protruding wedge separated South Germany more effectively from North Germany than the political frontier of the Main. Our South German allies showed the highest   20
degree of resolution, of national enthusiasm and dedication in seeing the threat to North Germany as theirs and wasting not a moment in acting with us. This was in spite of the immediate threat offered by a skilfully conducted campaign from the French side. We have seen for decades that France, in this dominating position, in this thrusting bastion which Strassburg presents against Germany,   25
has always succumbed to temptation whenever internal circumstances have made an external diversion useful.

H. Rothfels, *Bismarck und der Staat*, pp. 205–6†

1.5(a)   In his memoirs, Bismarck defends his editing and publishing of the Ems telegram, which led to the French declaration of war in 1870

If in execution of his Majesty's order I at once communicate this text, which contains no alteration in or addition to the telegram, not only to the newspapers, but also by telegraph to all our embassies, it will be known in Paris before midnight, and not only on account of its contents, but also on account of the manner of its distribution, will have the effect of a red rag upon the Gallic bull.   5
Fight we must if we do not want to act the part of the vanquished without a battle. Success, however, essentially depends upon the impression which the origination of the war makes upon us and others; it is important that we should be the party attacked and this [i.e. the party attacked] Gallic overweening and touchiness will make us if we announce in the face of Europe, so far as we can   10
without the speaking trumpet of the Reichstag, that we fearlessly meet the public threats of France.

Bismarck was recounting a conversation with Moltke, commander in chief of the Prussian army, and Roon, minister for war.

1.5(b)   Bismarck acknowledges his responsibility for the wars of 1864, 1866 and 1870

During the time that I was in office I advised three wars, the Danish, the Bohemian, and the French; but every time I first made myself clear whether the war, if it were successful, would bring a prize of victory worth the sacrifices which every war requires, and which are now so much greater than in the last century.

Otto von Bismarck, the Man and the Statesman, being the Reflections and Reminiscences of Otto Prince von Bismarck, Written and Dictated by Himself after His Retirement from Office, vol. 2 ed. A. J. Butler, pp. 100, 290

1.6   Heinrich Abeken, a member of the Prussian royal entourage, exults in the peace terms, in a letter to his wife, February 1871

That a peace was concluded such as has not been known in Germany for a thousand years, a peace before which that of 1815 is as nothing, may indeed be a cause of pride to you. And it has been gained by German power only, without any foreign help, and indeed, in spite of the envy and in opposition to the sympathies of foreign nations which have not dared to meddle with it. It is a   5
peace which gives back to Germany two strong fortresses, and a most beautiful province that will be grateful to us for having kept it from decay, and from falling into the hands of the devil of foreigners ...

Five billions of francs or fifteen hundred million thalers, are such a fabulous sum that no one can grasp it.

T. S. Hamerow, *The Age of Bismarck*, **p. 111**

1.7(a)　E. Jörg, a Catholic democrat, who was a member of the Bavarian Landtag and subsequently of the Centre Party in the Reichstag, opposes the Franco-Prussian War, 1 January 1871

Born out of a terrible struggle with its western neighbour, it [German Kaiserdom] must from the start prohibit every sort of interference and mediation. As it claims to be a pure nation-State yet still incomplete nation-State, it cannot, by its very nature, accept that its boundaries be defined by binding treaties; it must rather reserve the right to pull into its framework at the next favourable　　5 opportunity those areas of German nationality which stand outside it. Therefore it was no exaggeration but the truth when, months ago, it was proclaimed in Berlin that the new German Reich must be a *Weltreich*, strong enough to defeat, without alliances or treaties, not only any other power but a coalition of all foreign powers ...　　10

How is one reasonably supposed to picture the future relationship of Germany and France, in view of the abyss of irreconcilable hatred which has opened up between them; how are the two nations to find their way back to each other while the whole French people passes on its grim thirst for revenge to its children and children's children?

J. C. G. Röhl, *From Bismarck to Hitler*, **p. 24**

1.7(b)　Johann Jacoby, a lifelong democrat, opposes the annexation of Alsace-Lorraine

Gentlemen, do not let yourselves be led away by well-sounding words, and though they offer you the empire of the world, be not tempted to worship the idols of power. Test this well-sounding phrase, and you will find that it is nothing but a disguise for the old and barbarous right of force. Alsace and Lorraine, they say, were formerly German property, and must again become　　5 German. How so, we enquire? Have, then, Alsace and Lorraine no inhabitants? or are, perchance, the inhabitants of these provinces to be regarded as having no volition, as a thing that one may at once take possession of, and dispose of just as one likes? Have they lost all their rights through the war, have they become slaves, whose fate is at the arbitrary disposal of the conqueror? Even the most　　10 ardent and insatiate partisan of annexation allows that the inhabitants of Alsace and Lorraine are in heart and soul French. And however much they might have offended us, it would be contrary to all human justice should we try to

Germanize them compulsorily, and incorporate them against their will either with Prussia or any other German state.

Johann Jacoby was imprisoned for making this speech at a public gathering in the autumn of 1870.

T. S. Hamerow, *The Age of Bismarck*, p. 108

Questions

1 Compare the arguments used in **1.4** and **1.5(a)** and **1.5(b)** to justify the Franco-Prussian war.
2 How convincing, in the light of **1.7(a)** and **1.7(b)**, do you find Bismarck's justification for the annexation of Alsace-Lorraine in **1.4**?
3 In the light of **1.6**, **1.7(a)** and **1.7(b)** what was the significance of the Treaty of Frankfurt for the future of the German empire?

The constitution of the empire

The constitutional framework of the empire was a unique construction [**1.8**]. It was largely a reflection of Bismarck's ideas, modified where necessary to secure the approval of the rulers of Württemberg and Bavaria. In its main provisions the constitution was based on that of the North German Confederation, adopted in 1867. Though described as a federation containing twenty-two states and three free cities (see **1.8, Article 6**) the empire was inevitably dominated by Prussia, which contained three-fifths of the land area and three-fifths of the population. The imperial title was invested in the Prussian royal house. The imperial chancellor was to be appointed by the emperor; the chancellor's office was usually combined with those of prime minister and foreign minister of Prussia as well. Prussia was to have seventeen of the fifty-eight votes in the Bundesrat (the Upper House), sufficient to block any reform to the constitution.

If the empire was hardly a federation in the true sense of the word, nor was it a constitutional monarchy, despite its parliamentary institutions. The emperor's authority was considerable, when he chose to exercise it. He had the right to conduct foreign policy and to declare war (with the assent of the Bundesrat); he had absolute control of Prussia's armed forces, and of those of the rest of the empire in time of war, the *Kommandogewalt*; he had the right of appointment to all imperial as well as Prussian offices; he had the right to summon and, more importantly, to dissolve the Reichstag. In effect the emperor controlled the armed forces, the bureaucracy and the diplomacy of the new Germany. For the first twenty years of its history these powers were exercised by Bismarck, on behalf of Wilhelm I. When his grandson Wilhelm II, after the brief interlude of Friedrich III's reign, succeeded to the throne in 1888, a clash of authority became inevitable. But it was a clash between emperor and chancellor, not between monarch and parliament.

If it was not a constitutional monarchy, however, nor was the empire an absolutist one [1.8]. Some of the emperor's powers required the assent of the two assemblies that were inherited from the North German Confederation. The Bundesrat represented the princes of the empire and was rarely a barrier to the royal will. But the Reichstag, or Lower House, was elected on the basis of universal manhood suffrage for all over twenty-five, with a secret ballot. It had the right to approve all imperial legislation and the imperial budget. Under the terms of the constitution only indirect taxes could be imposed by the imperial government (and these needed the assent of the Reichstag). All direct taxation, such as income tax, was confined to the member states. The Reichstag had to meet every year.

Compared with the powers enjoyed by the British Houses of Parliament, those of the Reichstag do not seem noticeably inferior, but in two respects they were. Unlike the prime minister in Britain, the imperial chancellor's tenure of office depended exclusively on the will of the sovereign and not on the support of a majority in the Reichstag. Secondly, while Bismarck and his successors had the right to appear in the Reichstag, they could not be called to account there for the policies they were pursuing. Responsible government, in the sense of a government responsible to an elected assembly, was not a feature of the German constitution, nor was it ever intended to be.

Even though Germany anticipated Britain by some forty years in conceding universal manhood suffrage, this was not to be the gateway to democracy. Bismarck had observed in 1866 that 'At the moment of decision the masses will decide on the side of kingship, regardless of whether the latter happens to follow a liberal or conservative tendency ... May I indeed express it as a conviction based on long experience that the artificial system of indirect and class elections is much more dangerous than that of direct and general suffrage, because it prevents contact between the highest authority and the healthy elements that constitute the core and mass of the people. In a country with monarchical traditions and loyal sentiments, the general suffrage by eliminating the influence of the liberal bourgeois classes, will also lead to monarchical elections' (Craig, *Germany, 1866–1945*, p. 45).

The latent conservatism of a mass electorate would, it was hoped, under-mine the potential opposition of those constitutionally minded parliamen-tarians Bismarck so disliked. As members of the Reichstag were also unpaid, until 1906, it was further hoped to exclude the workers' own representatives. It should also be noted that in the lower house of the Prussian parliament the three class voting system, established in 1849, gave a grossly inflated representation to the wealthy minority. Those in the first, and wealthiest, class of taxpayers, while only 4% of the voting population, enjoyed as many votes as those in the largest and poorest class, some 84% of the voting pop-ulation. This system withstood all attempts to have it reformed and endured until the collapse of the empire in 1918.

1.8   The imperial constitution (extracts)

Preamble

His Majesty the King of Prussia in the name of the North German Confederation, His Majesty the King of Bavaria, His Majesty the King of Württemberg, His Royal Highness the Grand Duke of Baden and His Royal Highness the Grand Duke of Hesse and Rhenish Hesse for the areas of the   5
Grand Duchy of Hesse lying north of the Main, hereby establish a perpetual federation for the protection of the federation's territory, as well as for the maintenance of the welfare of the German people. This federation shall bear the name German Empire, and shall have the following:

Constitution   10

1. FEDERAL TERRITORY

ARTICLE 1. The federal territory consists of the states of Prussia (with Lauenburg), Bavaria, Saxony ... [see Article 6. for full list].

2. IMPERIAL LEGISLATION

ARTICLE 2. The Empire exercises the right of legislation within the federal   15
territory according to the provisions of this Constitution, and with the effect that imperial legislation shall take precedence over state legislation ...
ARTICLE 3. There shall be a common right of citizenship for all Germany, with the effect that every person (subject, citizen) residing in any federated state shall be treated as a member of any other federated state and shall be treated equally   20
in such matters as fixed residence, pursuit of a livelihood, eligibility for public office, acquiring of property, achievement of state citizenship, and enjoyment of special rights of citizenship ...
ARTICLE 5. The imperial legislative power shall be exercised by the Bundesrat and the Reichstag. The agreement of the majority votes of both bodies is   25
necessary and sufficient for an imperial statute.

3. BUNDESRAT

ARTICLE 6. The Bundesrat is composed of the representatives of the members of the federation, and the voting procedure shall be as follows: Prussia, together with the former votes of Hanover, Kurhesse, Holstein, Nassau, and Frankfurt, 17   30 votes; Bavaria, 6; Saxony, 4; Württemberg, 4; Baden, 3; Hesse, 3; Mecklenburg-Schwerin, 2; Brunswick, 2; Saxe-Weimar, 1; Mecklenburg-Strelitz, 1; Oldenburg, 1; Saxe-Meiningen, 1; Saxe-Altenburg, 1; Saxe-Coburg-Gotha, 1; Anhalt, 1; Schwarzburg-Rudolstadt, 1; Schwarzburg-Sondershausen, 1; Waldeck, 1; Reuss of the Elder Line, 1; Reuss of the Younger Line, 1; Schaumburg-Lippe, 1; Lippe, 1;   35 Lübeck, 1; Bremen, 1; Hamburg, 1. Total 58 votes.

Every member of the federation can name as many delegates to the Bundesrat as it has votes, but all delegations must cast their votes as a unit.

ARTICLE 9. Every member of the Bundesrat has the right to appear in the Reichstag ... No one can simultaneously be a member of the Bundesrat and the   40 Reichstag.

4. PRESIDING OFFICER

ARTICLE 11. The presiding officer of the federation shall be the King of Prussia, who shall bear the name *German Emperor*. The Emperor shall represent the Empire in the Law of Nations, declare war and conclude peace in the name   45 of the Empire, enter into alliances and other treaties with foreign states, and accredit and receive ambassadors.

The consent of the Bundesrat is required for a declaration of war in the name of the Empire, with the exception of cases of an attack upon the territory of the Empire or its coasts.   50

ARTICLE 12. The Emperor summons, opens, prorogues, and closes the Bundesrat and the Reichstag.

ARTICLE 13. The Bundesrat and the Reichstag shall be summoned annually ...

ARTICLE 14. The Bundesrat must be summoned immediately after such a demand by one third of its membership.   55

ARTICLE 15. The presiding chair in the Bundesrat and the conduct of business appertain to the Imperial Chancellor who is to be appointed by the Emperor ...

5. REICHSTAG

ARTICLE 20. The Reichstag shall be elected by universal and direct elections with secret voting ...   60

ARTICLE 22. The meetings of the Reichstag shall be public ...

ARTICLE 24. The legislative period of the Reichstag lasts five years. For the dissolution of the Reichstag during this period a resolution of the Bundesrat with the concurrence of the Emperor is required ...

ARTICLE 28. The Reichstag acts with an absolute majority. The presence of a   65 majority of the legal number of members is required for the validity of its action ...

ARTICLE 78. Amendments of the Constitution are made by way of legislation. They shall be considered as rejected if they have fourteen votes against them in the Bundesrat.

L. L. Snyder, *Documents of German History*, pp. 226–30

Questions

1 How far did the German constitution of 1871 display the features of a federal system of government?
2 'A princely insurance institute against democracy' (Wilhelm Liebknecht). Discuss this verdict on the German constitution of 1871.
3 In what respects did the constitution of 1871 guarantee the primacy of Prussia in the German empire?

The German economy, 1871–90

The period of Bismarck's chancellorship was one of unprecedented, if uneven, economic growth. The German industrial revolution began later than those of Britain, Belgium and France, but by the end of the century Germany had taken the lead in many areas of heavy industry, notably steel production, and had also laid the foundations of German supremacy in fields such as chemicals and electrical engineering.

These economic changes were accompanied by many of the features characteristic of industrial revolutions elsewhere: a rapid growth in the population, a movement from the countryside to the towns, a dramatic increase in external trade and changes to the class structure, to mention only the most obvious. Where perhaps the German experience was unusual was in the extent and the rapidity of the changes. During the British industrial revolution annual growth rates had rarely exceeded 2%. In Germany they not infrequently reached 7–8%. Coal, iron and steel production all trebled their outputs between 1871 and 1891. The population expanded by 8 million over the same period, while the labour force grew from 18 million to 23 million between 1875 and 1895.

At the same time it would be wrong to assume that such changes took place evenly, or that they transformed all areas of the German economy. There was a serious economic crisis in 1873 which led to a long period of deflation and falling prices, ending only in 1879. A brief recovery was followed by another, shallower depression which did not end until 1886. According to Wehler, 'In the twenty-odd years of Bismarck's chancellorship, there were, therefore, only four years of economic boom' (Wehler, *The German Empire*, p. 34).

Similarly, while industry's share of national output overtook that of agriculture in 1895, the agricultural work-force actually increased until 1913 and agricultural lobbies continued to exercise an influential role in German politics right up to 1914.

The economic changes that did occur had powerful political and social consequences. There was firstly a significant increase in the size of the industrial proletariat. The industrial revolution also promoted the growth of new elites whose wealth was based on commerce and industry rather than on the ownership of land or service to the state. German political life came to reflect these changes in the class structure. The growth of the Social Democratic Party was a direct result of industrialisation as was the clash between agricultural and industrial interests over tariffs. Economic fluctuations, when they occurred, had the effect of uniting the middle and upper classes in their hostility to socialism, while raising the political temperature. The internal tensions brought about by these economic changes put a considerable strain on Germany's political institutions and they provide the backcloth against which political developments in the Bismarckian era need to be seen. 1.9–1.11 provide statistical evidence for some of these changes and their social consequences.

1.9 Germany's economic growth in comparison with her rivals

	1860	1870	1880	1890	1900	1910
(a) Coal production (million tons)						
Germany	12	34	59	89	149	222
France	8.3	13.3	19.4	26.1	33.4	38.4
Britain	81	112	149	184	228	268
Russia	0.15	0.75	3.2	6	16.2	24.9
(b) Pig iron production (million tons)						
Germany		1.3	2.5	4.1	7.5	9.5
France		1.2	1.7	2	2.7	4
Britain	3.9	6	7.8	8	9	10
Russia		0.4	0.4	0.9	2.9	3
(c) Steel production (million tons)						
Germany		0.3	0.7	2.3	6.7	13.8
France		0.3	0.4	0.7	1.6	3.4
Britain		0.7	1.3	3.6	5	5.9
Russia				0.4	1.5	3.5

A. J. P. Taylor, *The Struggle for Mastery in Europe*, pp. xxix–xxx

1.10 Structure of the labour force in occupational groups, 1875–1913

Sector	1875	1885	1895	1905	1913
Agriculture	9,230	9,700	9,788	9,926	10,701
Mining	286	354	432	665	863
Industry and handicraft	5,153	6,005	7,524	9,572	10,857
Transport	349	461	620	901	1,174
Commerce/Banking	1,116	1,457	1,960	2,806	3,474
Insurance, hotels domestic service	(1,490)	1,488	1,571	1,541	1,542
Other services	589	659	894	1,159	1,493
Defence	430	462	606	651	864
Total	18,643	20,577	23,405	27,221	30,968

V. R. Berghahn, *Modern Germany*, p. 282

1.11 Growth of some major cities, 1875–1910 (000s)

	1875	1890	1910
Berlin	967	1588	2071
Bremen	103	126	217
Cologne	135	282	516
Dortmund	58	90	214
Dresden	197	276	548
Duisburg	37	59	229
Düsseldorf	81	145	359
Essen	55	79	295
Frankfurt	103	180	414
Hamburg	265	324	931
Kiel	37	69	212
Leipzig	127	295	590
Munich	193	349	596
Nuremberg	91	142	333
Stuttgart	107	140	286

V. R. Berghahn, *Modern Germany*, p. 272

Questions

1 Compare the rates of growth of the German coal, iron and steel industries with those of her European rivals [1.9].
2 Which sectors of employment showed (a) the greatest and (b) the least proportional change between 1875 and 1913 in Germany [1.10]?
3 Which sectors of employment showed the greatest absolute increases?
4 Which German cities listed in 1.11 can trace their growth to changes in mining and industry?
5 How far do 1.9, 1.10 and 1.11 bear out the view that by 1913 Germany was a mature industrial economy?

1.12 Housing conditions in German cities

In Berlin conditions are specially bad, and the average number of persons inhabiting one tenement (*Grundstück*) has risen from 60.7 in 1880 to 66.0 in 1885. Subletting was shown by the census of 1880 to be exceedingly frequent, 7.1 per cent of the population took in persons who boarded and lodged with them, and 15.3 per cent took in persons to sleep (*Schlafleute*). One instance is given of a

5

household taking 34 such night lodgers, in another case there were eleven, including two women. Thirty eight per cent of the families taking night lodgers lived in a single room; one instance is mentioned in which a man and his wife shared their room with seven men and one woman. Though the worst of night shelters, known as 'Pennen', have now been suppressed by the police, it is still   10
'the opinion of experienced observers ... that the evils existing in the large towns of England are less crying than in Germany'.

Royal Commission on Labour, *Foreign Reports: Germany* **(London 1893), pp. 104–5, cited in T. S. Hamerow,** *The Age of Bismarck,* **pp. 179–80**

1.13   The social consequences of industrialisation

Our era is saddled with social classes that are deprived and neglected and have been abused for centuries. Suddenly left to themselves and exposed to the competitive struggle, these classes necessarily were left behind to the same extent as those who were better situated, the more educated and the propertied classes, advanced more quickly. Small industry could not compete with large. Modern   5
technology was available only to large-scale capital. The enormous increase in production and trade did not benefit all classes equally but mainly a privileged minority. Until a few years ago wages in Germany lagged dangerously behind the general movement of prices. Even apart from this, the effects of big industry on living, education and family conditions were in any case predominantly   10
unfavourable. It was the working class, thousands of members of which were suddenly dismissed, who suffered most from economic crises. The same worker who was daily receiving new political rights, who on all sides was being summoned into the new political arena, who was assured every day that he was the real people – this same worker until not very long ago found himself, for the   15
most part, worse off every day. The moment was bound to come when he would say to himself: it seems that in political life in serving my country, I am to count for as much as the noblest and richest, but in economic and social life the gap is not only to continue but is to be widened.

Gustav Schmoller, *The Social Question and the Prussian State* **(1874) cited in W. M. Simon,** *Germany in the Age of Bismarck,* **p. 188**

1.14   The consequences of economic instability

He [Bleichröder] had anticipated a crash and had warned Bismarck that the sudden collapse of the Vienna market in May 1873 was likely to affect Berlin as well. By the summer and fall of 1873, the stock markets of New York and Berlin suffered calamitous losses, credit became scarce, and businesses began to fail. In the early days of 1874, 61 banks, 116 industrial enterprises, and 4 railway   5
companies announced their bankruptcies.

To the surprise of many people, Bleichröder included, the crash turned into the longest and most pervasive depression of the century. Prices, profits and dividends dropped precipitously; production declined and unemployment increased. The losses people suffered were catastrophic and often had a crippling   10 effect on families for decades to come ...

The crash and the ensuing depression had a profound effect on society. It dramatized, as nothing before had, the changed nature of that society. It demonstrated that Germany had become a capitalistic country, despite the pre-capitalist ethos that still prevailed. Among the public at large there was a   15 strong tendency to translate the crash into moral terms, as punishment for wrongdoing ... Conservative and Catholic critics turned this moralizing tendency into a full-scale attack against laissez-faire Manchesterism, blaming liberals and Jews for the plight of the country. Capitalism of course survived, but it was a curiously suspect or devalued capitalism; in Germany after 1873, in good years   20 and bad years, there was always a powerful anti-capitalist sentiment – which the left and right shared. At the same time, the long crisis led to the mobilization of economic interests, which also demanded a change in the government's liberal policy.

F. Stern, *Gold and Iron*, pp. 182–3

Questions

1   Explain the term 'laissez-faire Manchesterism' [**1.14, line 18**].
2   How far do **1.12** and **1.13** suggest that the working classes in Germany were the victims rather than the beneficiaries of economic growth, and if so, how is this to be explained?
3   Why should the right and left have shared 'a powerful anti-capitalist sentiment' after 1873 [**1.14, line 21**]?
4   What political consequences, in your view, were likely to follow from the economic changes that took place in Germany between 1875 and 1913?

2 Bismarck's rule at home

Bismarck has been accused of setting up a chancellor-dictatorship and in this way acting as 'the evil godfather of the Third Reich' (Martel, *Modern Germany Reconsidered*, pp. 38–40). The indictment rests upon four main charges: first that by his determination to grasp and retain all political power in his own hands he denied to the Reichstag any role in the formation of governments and hence effectively prevented the emergence of a constitutional monarchy in Germany; secondly that by characterising all his political opponents as *Reichsfeinde* (enemies of the empire), he tarnished opposition to his regime with the stain of disloyalty, and thus excluded large elements of the population, notably Catholics and Social Democrats, from the political process; and thirdly that by allying himself to conservative elites in the latter stages of his career he prevented the passage of much needed social and political reforms and diverted German economic policy on to a protectionist and nationalistic course. Finally, the legacy of Bismarck's rule, it has been argued, was a German political system ill-equipped to meet the internal and external problems that faced the empire after his departure. It is the purpose of this chapter to examine the first three of these charges. The final one is reserved for Chapter 4.

Bismarck's chancellor-dictatorship

Despite his frequent threats of resignation, Bismarck never seems to have doubted his own indispensability as chancellor, and even after his dismissal in 1890 intrigued to secure his way back to power. Wehler has described his rule as a kind of Bonapartism, resting as it did on 'a combination of charismatic, plebiscitary and traditional elements' (Wehler, *The German Empire*, p. 57). The concept of Bonapartism is derived from Napoleon III's rule in France. Wehler argues that the dictatorial rule which characterised both regimes was 'accepted, indeed demanded, by the ruling class on the grounds of its need for protection' (p. 58). By way of comparison, in a recent biography Gall states that 'the objectives he [Bismarck] pursued were often shortwindedly as well as short-sightedly conceived, the only purposes they served being the acquisition and the preservation of power' (*Bismarck*, p. 234).

But Bismarck had not only to retain the confidence of the emperor (a dependence of which he became acutely aware after the death of Wilhelm I in 1888); he also had to work within the parameters of the constitution he himself had designed. This gave the Reichstag the undoubted right to approve the indirect taxes on which the empire depended and such legislation as the chancellor wished to pass. The nature of Bismarck's authority is thus directly related to his handling of the Reichstag and the political parties who were represented there. Bismarck had little faith in parliamentary democracy. But while he did very little to encourage the Reichstag, some responsibility must also lie with the elected politicians and the parties which they represented for the opportunities missed, and the willingness at times to sacrifice the rights, whether of the Catholic church or of the Social Democratic Party, for the sake of national unity and security. Wehler has gone so far as to accuse the parties of displaying 'in their practical use of tactics a high degree of cringing conformity towards the existing structures of power' (*The German Empire*, p. 72).

The concept of a recognised opposition, licensed to criticise and, if successful electorally, able to replace the existing government, was both bitterly opposed by Bismarck and difficult to operate in a multi-party system. Such a party system was a feature of the Reichstag throughout the history of the empire. In 1871 there were four distinctive party groupings. First, on the right were the traditional Conservatives, mainly based in the eastern provinces of Prussia, and drawing support from the aristocracy, the army, the bureaucracy and the Protestant clergy; allied to them were the Free Conservatives, who were Bismarck's closest and most consistent supporters. The second group, the National Liberal Party, was formed out of the Hanoverian Liberal Party, founded by Rudolf von Bennigsen, and those members of the Prussian Progressive Party who had abandoned their opposition to Bismarck in 1866 at the time of the Austro-Prussian war. The Progressive Party, the third grouping, remained truer to their liberal convictions, but shared with the National Liberals a commitment to free trade and German unification. The final group, the Catholic Centre Party, was founded in 1870, specifically to represent the Catholic interest, now greatly increased by the inclusion of the South German states within the empire. At its most successful the Centre party attracted the support of over 80% of Catholic voters. These four parties were soon joined by a fifth, the German Socialist Working Men's Party, later known as the SPD. This came into existence in 1875 as the result of a merger between the moderate

General German Working Men's Society, founded by Ferdinand Lassalle in 1861, and the Marxist Social Democratic Working Men's Party, founded by August Bebel and Wilhelm Liebknecht in 1871.

All the parties that sat in the Reichstag accepted the Constitution of 1871 and were prepared to work within its boundaries, though they differed in their enthusiasm for it. Bismarck refused to identify himself with any one of them and preferred to remain above the battle. He was never prepared to accept the right of the Reichstag to determine the composition of the imperial government, or to affect his own position as its head. How far he valued the process of debate and was prepared to accept the need for the Reichstag at all can perhaps be judged from the documents which follow.

2.1 Bismarck's reflections on absolutism, written at the beginning of his retirement, 1890–1

Absolutism would be the ideal constitution for European states if the king and his Ministers were not like all other men, to whom it is not given to rule with superhuman knowledge, insight and justice. The most perceptive and well-intentioned absolute rulers succumb to human weakness and incompetence as they do to the over estimation of their own insight, to the influence and   5
eloquence of favourites, not to mention the influence of wives and mistresses. The monarchy and the ideal monarch, if his best intentions are not to become harmful, needs the sharp thorns of criticism if he is not to be in danger of losing his way. Joseph II provides a salutary example.

Criticism can only be exercised through a free press and parliaments in their   10
modern sense. Both correctives can have their effectiveness blunted and finally lost through misuse. To prevent this is one of the tasks of a conserving policy which cannot be accomplished without a struggle with parliament and press. The drawing of the boundaries within which this struggle must be contained is a matter of political tact and judgement if the check essential to government is   15
neither to be impeded nor to predominate. I do not regard absolutism as a form of government which can be successful in the long term for Germany. The Prussian constitution, apart from a few clauses translated from the Belgian one, is sensible in its main principle. It has three elements, the King and two Chambers, each of which can by its vote prevent arbitrary changes to the lawful status quo.   20
Therein lies a proper distribution of legislative power. If this is freed from the open criticism of the press and from the scrutiny of parliament, then the danger that it will be misdirected is increased. The absolutism of the Crown is no more tolerable than the absolutism of parliamentary majorities.

H. Rothfels, *Bismarck und der Staat*, pp. 298–9†

2.2 Bismarck's private views of political parties as reported by Prince von Bülow

IN MY [Bülow's] PRESENCE and in the bosom of the family, he expressed some violent opinions of his domestic enemies. He did not want in the least to govern autocratically, he said, although the reproach was daily levelled against him. Real autocracy would be very different from the present government in Germany. He was perfectly well aware that, in Germany, in the second half of   5
the nineteenth century, absolutism and autocracy would be impossible, apart from the fact that such government had never been one of his ideals. But a parliamentary regime seemed to him just impossible. Our parties possessed neither the patriotism of the French nor the sound common sense of the English. Under the circumstances he did not understand what benefits the German   10
Liberals promised themselves from the 'inauguration of responsible ministries of the realm', which they had lately adopted as part of their programme. As long as he remained in office he would never countenance such a thing. Considering the political incapacity of the average German, the intellectual parliamentary system would lead to conditions such as had prevailed in 1848, that is to say, to   15
weakness and incompetence on the top, and to bumptiousness and ever new demands from below.

Prince Bernhard von Bülow was a professional diplomat from 1873 to 1898; he became foreign secretary in 1898 then chancellor from 1900 to 1909.

Memoirs of Prince von Bülow, vol. 4, p. 558, cited in T. S. Hamerow, *The Age of Bismarck*, p. 297

2.3 Critics of Bismarck's rule

2.3(a) Princess Victoria, daughter of Queen Victoria and wife of the Crown Prince Friedrich who briefly succeeded Wilhelm I as emperor in 1888, in a letter written to Queen Victoria between 1887 and 1889

What a blessed thing it would be if this regime of Bismarck's omnipotence were not to last for ever, if other motives and sentiments and another spirit were to pervade the German government. B. is a very great man, a man of genius and power, does his best and has done great things for his country. One must be just and grateful, but as you cannot gather grapes of thorns or figs of thistles, so can   5
you not expect from him that which Germany lacks, and which it thirsts for, and that is peace among its classes, races, religions and parties, good and friendly relations with its neighbours, liberty and the respect of right instead of force, and the protection of the weak against the oppression of the strong.

T. S. Hamerow, *The Age of Bismarck*, p. 157

2.3(b)   Notes for a speech in February 1881, by Rudolph Haym, philosopher, historian and a National Liberal member of the Reichstag

By and large, Prince Bismarck represents for me the incarnation of the state. I do not always like his methods. Sometimes – I have in mind particularly universal and equal suffrage – he has gone too far in the direction of liberalism for my taste, at other times he has regrettable tendencies towards conservatism, at yet other times he encourages interest-group politics which appeals to egoism and   5
therefore slights the nobler motives in political life and must have a confusing and even corrupting effect. But in the face of all this I remind myself that nobody else has such a lively regard for the idea of making the young empire vital, permanent and resilient, and that he is untiringly and successfully at work to realise this ideal with sensible realism according to circumstances.

W. M. Simon, *Germany in the Age of Bismarck*, p. 222

Questions

1   Why did Bismarck reject both the 'absolutism of the crown' and 'the absolutism of parliamentary majorities' [2.1]?
2   Is it possible to reconcile the views expressed by Bismarck in **2.1** and **2.2** about the value of parliaments?
3   How far do **2.3(a)** and **2.3(b)** agree in their perceptions of Bismarck's rule and where do they differ?
4   How far do **2.1** to **2.3** suggest that Bismarck believed in his own political capacity but not in that of anyone else?

Bismarck and the *Kulturkampf*

The *Kulturkampf* is the name traditionally given to the conflict between Bismarck and the Catholic Church that raged throughout the 1870s and really only came to an end in 1885. The conflict acquired its name in a speech delivered by a left-liberal deputy, Rudolf Virchow, in the Reichstag in 1872. Virchow, as well as being a politician, was a renowned scientist of rationalist views. In 1865 he had strongly opposed Bismarck's determination to collect taxes without the approval of the budget by the Prussian Diet, and Bismarck had even challenged him to a duel for questioning his veracity. In the *Kulturkampf* Virchow and Bismarck were on the same side, Virchow claiming that 'the struggle against the Roman Church was, with every day that passed, acquiring more and more "the character of a great struggle for civilisation (*Kulturkampf*) in the interests of humanity"' (Craig, *Germany*,

1866–1945, p. 74). That a leading liberal politician could present the campaign against the Catholic Church, which dominated the 1870s, as 'a struggle for civilisation' is one of the paradoxes of the *Kulturkampf*. Another is the curious alliance that developed between Bismarck and his erstwhile liberal opponents in that struggle.

There were many facets to the *Kulturkampf*. To free thinkers such as Virchow, Catholicism in the 1870s could indeed seem a reactionary and obscurantist creed. In 1854 Pope Pius IX proclaimed in a papal bull the dogma of the Immaculate Conception of the Blessed Virgin Mary, without scriptural authority to support it, and without reference to a General Council. In 1864 he issued a Syllabus of Errors, condemning what were seen to be a wide range of modernist heresies, including Socialism and Liberalism. It concluded with the notorious 80th Proposal: 'Whosoever teaches that the Roman Pontiff ought to reconcile himself and adjust himself with progress, liberalism and modern civilisation ... let him be anathema' (B. and M. Pawley, *Rome and Canterbury through the Centuries*, p. 210). Finally, in 1870 the Vatican Council, meeting in Rome just as the Pope's temporal possessions were being wrested from him, restored the balance by proclaiming the dogma of papal infallibility [2.4]. Though the doctrine was approved by 451 votes to 88, with 62 conditional acceptances, it led to the defection of several German Catholics, including the distinguished Bavarian theologian, Ignaz Döllinger. National Liberals such as Virchow were only too ready to see in these claims a campaign against freedom of thought and a bid for papal supremacy.

Bismarck's motives for supporting the liberal opposition to Catholicism are harder to gauge. He was no friend to liberty, or to Virchow's philosophical materialism. But he certainly distrusted the supra-national claims of Catholicism and hence the doubtful loyalty, as he saw it, of German Catholics to the new empire. He feared the influence of Catholicism in promoting anti-German sentiment in Alsace-Lorraine and eastern Prussia. He detested the notion of confessional political parties such as the Centre Party. He suspected the enlightened social teaching of men such as Ketteler, bishop of Mainz. But he was also sufficiently an opportunist to use the *Kulturkampf* to improve his relations with the National Liberal Party, and to bring it to a halt when it proved an embarrassment rather than a source of strength.

The struggle began in January 1871 when Bismarck brought to an end the Catholic Section of the Prussian Ministry of Culture. This organisation had been set up in 1841 to represent the interests of Catholics in Lutheran Prussia, and for thirty years had functioned effectively. In February 1871

Bismarck received a request from Bishop Ketteler, supported by fifty-six Catholic members of the Prussian Lower House, the House of Deputies, that the new Germany should support the restoration of the Papal states. To Bismarck this was an unwarranted attempt to influence policy by a Catholic party. The new Reichstag when it convened in June was similarly unwilling to accept a Centre Party request that basic rights specifically for the Catholic Church should be incorporated into the imperial constitution.

The real campaign got under way in January 1872 with the appointment of Adalbert Falk, a committed liberal in religious matters, to head the Prussian Ministry of Culture, with Bismarck's distinct instructions that he was 'to re-establish the rights of the Church vis-à-vis the state' (Gall, *Bismarck*, p. 24). Falk duly introduced a Schools Inspection Law, placing all Prussian schools under lay rather than clerical control. In practice such control was largely confined to Prussia's eastern provinces. In July 1872 measures were introduced both into the Prussian Landtag and the imperial Reichstag banning the Jesuit movement, long suspected of promoting Polish nationalism, from Germany. This ban was to last until the middle of the First World War. These measures provoked papal opposition and led to Bismarck's most famous utterance in the *Kulturkampf*. The particular issue was the pope's refusal to accept as the German delegate to the Holy See Bismarck's nominee, Cardinal Prince Gustav von Hohenlohe-Schillingsfürst, a renowned opponent of the Jesuits and a member of the Catholic hierarchy. In an angry debate in the Reichstag at which members urged Bismarck to break off all relations with the papacy, the chancellor refused to go that far, but reassured his hearers: 'Have no fear: we shall not go to Canossa – either in body or in spirit.' (The reference to Canossa was a deliberate comparison with the occasion when the Holy Roman Emperor Henry IV had been made to do penance for three days in the winter of 1077 by Pope Gregory V for interfering with papal appointments.)

The *Kulturkampf* reached a peak in 1873–5. The May Laws passed in 1873 prescribed the training that all Catholic priests must receive, notably in philosophy, history and German literature, transferred disciplinary authority over the Church to state agencies and made civil marriage compulsory. When the papacy threatened with excommunication those who complied with the laws, Falk responded by dismissing, and in some cases imprisoning, those who refused to accept them. By 1876 1,400 parishes in Prussia, one third of the total, were without incumbents. In 1875 the ban on Jesuits was extended to all religious orders except those engaged in medical service.

Far from crushing the influence of the Catholic Church and the Centre Party, these measures only served to strengthen it. The Centre Party doubled its representation in the Prussian House of Deputies in 1873 and in the Reichstag in 1874. Bismarck lost the support of many Conservatives and Lutherans who, while refusing to come to the defence of their fellow Christians, did not welcome the secular tendencies which the *Kulturkampf* encouraged. With the election of a new Pope, Leo XIII, in 1878, there was an opportunity for reconciliation. Bismarck was also by now seeking new political allies to support his attack on socialism and his new tariff policy. Bit by bit, the campaign against Catholicism was allowed to wane. The most objectionable of the May Laws were finally repealed in 1885. Good relations were renewed with the papacy. Overtures were made to the Centre Party to win support for Bismarck's economic measures and Bismarck even contemplated a deal with Windhorst, the Centre Party leader, in 1890. With hindsight the *Kulturkampf* can be seen to have proved neither effective nor necessary. The following documents indicate some of the reasons why nonetheless it happened, and why Bismarck supported it.

2.4 The dogma of papal infallibility, July 1870

We teach and define that it is a dogma divinely revealed: that the Roman Pontiff, when he speaks *ex cathedra*, that is when in discharge of the office of Pastor and Doctor of all Christians, by virtue of his supreme Apostolic authority, he defines a doctrine regarding faith or morals to be held by the Universal Church, by the divine assistance promised to him in blessed Peter, is possessed of that infallibility   5 with which the divine Redeemer willed that His Church should be endowed for defining doctrine regarding faith or morals: and that therefore such definitions of the Roman Pontiff are irreformable of themselves, and not from the consent of the Church.

But if anyone – which may God avert – presume to contradict this Our   10 definition let him be anathema.

B. and M. Pawley, *Rome and Canterbury*, p. 228

2.5   A cartoon from *Kladderadatsch*, 1875

Zwischen Berlin und Rom.

Der letzte Zug war mir allerdings unangenehm; aber die Partie ist deshalb noch nicht verloren. Ich habe noch einen sehr schönen Zug in petto!

Das wird auch der letzte sein, und dann sind Sie in wenigen Zügen matt — — wenigitens für Deutschland.

Kladderadatsch *was a satirical German magazine. Its title means literally 'crash, bang, wallop'.*

Explain the 'pieces' on the chessboard:
a) Syllabus b) Encycl c) Kloster-Gesetz d) Interdict e) W

2.6   A speech by Bismarck to the Upper House of the Prussian Landtag, 10 March 1873

The question before us is, in my opinion, distorted, and the light in which we see it is a false one, if we regard it as a religious ecclesiastical question. It is essentially a political question. It is not, as our Catholic citizens are being persuaded, a matter of a struggle between belief and unbelief, it is a matter of the conflict, which is as old as the human race, between monarchy and priesthood, a conflict that goes back even beyond the appearance of our Saviour in this world ... the conflict which under the name of the struggle between the popes and emperors occupied German medieval history to the point of the disintegration of the German Empire ...

  What is at stake is the defence of the state, it is a matter of delimiting the scope of domination of priests and of kings, and this limitation must be drawn so

5

10

that the state can maintain itself, for in the realm of this world the state has the paramount power ...

Where conditions are favourable it is possible to have a dualistic constitution in a country; the Austro-Hungarian state is an illustration of this. But no 15 confessional dualism is to be found there; but here what is at issue is the establishment of two confessional states that would necessarily find themselves in a position of dualistic conflict, one of which would have as its sovereign ruler a foreign ecclesiastical prince whose seat is in Rome, a prince who because of the recent changes in the constitution of the Catholic Church is more powerful than 20 he used to be. If this programme had been realised we would therefore have had, instead of the unitary Prussian state, instead of the German Empire which was in the course of development, two political organisms running in parallel: one with its general staff in the Centre Party, the other with its general staff in the government and person of His Majesty the Emperor. This situation was a totally 25 unacceptable one for the government; and it was its duty to defend the state against this danger.

W. M. Simon, *Germany in the Age of Bismarck*, pp. 169–71

2.7 From Bismarck's speech to the Reichstag, 3 December 1884

I was drawn into this whole struggle [the *Kulturkampf*] only through the Polish side of the question. Twenty years ago I thought exactly as I do today that one can allow great latitude in German-speaking areas. But I was drawn into the struggle at that time because overwhelming evidence was presented to me that under the leadership of the priesthood, notably in West Prussia but also in 5 Silesia, Germans were being polonised. In West Prussia this had the consequence that the grandchildren of grandparents who were undoubtedly German, of German birth, with German names, no longer knew that they were German, could no longer speak German and thought of themselves as Polish. When I had more time to devote to the matter, I had the distinct impression that this whole 10 polonising activity of the priesthood had its point of origin in Berlin when the Catholic department [of the Ministry of Culture] at that time for its part was under the influence of Polish magnates.

H. Rothfels, *Bismarck und der Staat*, p. 245†

2.8 Bismarck's remarks in a cabinet meeting, 14 February 1886

I am a Bible believing Christian, but the enemy of priestly rule. This conflict is as old as the world and Lutheran pastors have as much inclination to play at being Pope as Catholic priests.

H. Rothfels, *Bismarck und der Staat*, p. 245†

Questions

1 How far do **2.4** and **2.5** suggest that the *Kulturkampf* was essentially a struggle about papal authority?
2 Why is Bismarck prepared in **2.6** to concede a dualistic constitution in Austria-Hungary but not in Germany? How valid are his arguments?
3 Compare the reasons for the *Kulturkampf* advanced in **2.6** and **2.7**. Which seem to you the more plausible?
4 How far does **2.8** help to explain Bismarck's policies towards the Catholic Church?

Bismarck and the socialist threat

While Bismarck eventually reached an accommodation with the Catholic Church he remained an inveterate opponent of socialism and the Social Democratic Party. He was to spend his last days in office trying to strengthen the Anti-Socialist Law which he had himself introduced in 1878.

What was the nature of the threat posed by the Social Democratic Party, and how serious was it? In order to answer this question one must attempt to distinguish between ends and means. Even the most moderate of German socialists attacked what they saw as the disastrous consequences of capitalism such as 'the iron law of wages', under which the workers were exploited by the owners of capital [2.9]. The Gotha Programme of 1875 [2.11] demanded 'the transformation of the means of production into the common property of society'. Most Social Democrats accepted the marxist critique of capitalism, and would thus have supported the marxist goal of a classless society. When it came to the methods for achieving this goal there was less agreement. One of the earliest German socialists, Ferdinand Lassalle, urged universal suffrage as the essential prerequisite; Wilhelm Liebknecht was a good deal less sanguine about its efficacy [2.10]. Both he and August Bebel went on to record their support for the Paris Commune of 1871 when French workers in Paris had briefly seized power from the hands of the de facto government then based at Tours, and this Bismarck never forgot nor forgave.

But in practice there was no evidence of conspiratorial activity among German socialists. Despite the efforts made to blame the two attempts to assassinate Emperor Wilhelm I in 1878 on the socialists, nothing was ever discovered to link these episodes to them. The first would-be assassin was Max Hodel, a half-crazed plumber, the second was Dr Karl Nobiling, an academic agronomist who was also mentally unbalanced. When in 1880 two

Social Democrats, Johann Most and Wilhelm Hasselmann, declared their sympathy for the policy of direct action which had just been adopted by the Russian anarchists, and which would result in the assassination of Tsar Alexander II in 1881, both men were expelled from the German Social Democratic Party.

Bismarck refused to be reassured. Following the first assassination attempt on Wilhelm I on 11 May 1878 he immediately presented the Reichstag with a draconian Anti-Socialist Bill. On this occasion it was decisively rejected, by 251 votes to 57. The National Liberal leader, Rudolf von Bennigsen, spoke for the majority: 'We ought more than ever to avoid mounting attacks against our political opponents as if they had sinned against the Common Good' (Gall, *Bismarck*, p. 94). Fate came to Bismarck's aid. On 2 June a second attempt was made to kill the emperor, seriously wounding him. Bismarck seized the opportunity to call a general election which resulted in the conservative parties gaining 29 new seats. More disastrously, the National Liberals now swallowed their scruples and voted as a bloc for the new Anti-Socialist Law, albeit with minor modifications [2.13]. This denial of principle was to cost the party dear. The Anti-Socialist Law was initially only to last for two and a half years, but it was successively renewed until 1890. In his last year as chancellor Bismarck even sought to extend it indefinitely and to add a clause permitting the expulsion of socialist agitators not only from their homes but from the country. Bismarck never lost his fear of socialism. **2.9–2.13** illustrate what Bismarck had to fear from the Social Democratic Party and the steps he took to contain the threat, real or illusory, which it presented.

2.9 Open letter from Ferdinand Lassalle to the Central Committee for the Summoning of a General Working Men's Congress at Leipzig, 1863

To make the working class their own employers – that is the means, the only means by which [the] inexorable and cruel law which determines wages can be abolished. When the working class is its own employer, the distinction between wages and profits will disappear, and the total yield of industry will take place, as the reward of labour, of the bare living wage ...

The universal and direct franchise is, as now appears, not merely your political principle – it is your social principle, the fundamental principle of all social advancement. It is the only means for improving the material condition of the working class.

T. S. Hamerow, *The Age of Bismarck*, pp. 215–16

2.10   Wilhelm Liebknecht, *Socialism: What it is and what it seeks to accomplish*, 1875

The tyrannous manner of production has overturned the natural relation between capital and labour and made labour the slave of capital. Is our wage labour not slavery? Is the modern wage labourer, because he can change his master, in any regard more free than the ancient slave? Does not hunger fasten him more firmly and more mercilessly to labour than the strongest iron chain? Yet our opponents   5
often rejoin: 'The worker is in a better condition today than in the last century.' Whether the assertion is true or false we leave undebated. Even if true it would prove nothing. It is not better position the socialist worker demands, but equal position. He will work no longer for another; he insists that each shall enjoy in equal measure the fruits of labour and the blessings of culture. He has enough   10
logic and sense of justice to lay no claim to a favoured place; he will also, however, accept no inferior one.

The continuance of the present manner of production is not consistent with the continuance of society. The great capitalist production was an advance. It has however become an obstruction. It no longer satisfies the economic needs of   15
society, and by society we mean not the small minority of privileged persons who are pleased to call themselves 'society', but the whole people ...

The present manner of production, resting on the basis of the wage system, has as a result on the one hand the accumulation of property in the hands of a few and the corruption of these few as a result of excessive possessions; on the   20
other hand, there is impoverishment of the masses and pauperism ...

'Down with the wage system!' That is the fundamental demand of social democracy – the Alpha and Omega of our agitation. Cooperative labour and association shall take the place of the wage system with its class rule.

T. S. Hamerow, *The Age of Bismarck*, p. 226

2.11   The Gotha Programme of the Socialist Labour Party of Germany

I

The emancipation of labour must be the work of the labouring class, opposed to which all other classes are a reactionary body.

II

Proceeding from this principle the Socialist Labour Party of Germany seeks   5
through all legal means the free state and the socialist society, the destruction of the iron law of wages, the overthrow of exploitation in all its forms and the abolition of all social and political inequality ...

The Socialist Labour Party of Germany demands as the foundation of the state: 10
1. Universal, equal and direct suffrage, with secret, obligatory voting by all citizens at all elections in state or community.

2. Direct legislation by the people. Decision as to peace or war by the people.
3. Common right to bear arms. Militia instead of the standing army.
4. Abolition of all laws of exception, especially all laws restricting the freedom of   15
the press, of association and assemblage; above all, all laws restricting the
freedom of public opinion, thought and investigation.
5. Legal judgment through the people.
6. Universal and equal popular education by the state. Universal and compulsory
education. Free instruction in all forms of art. Declaration that religion is a   20
private matter.
The Socialist Labour Party of Germany demands within the present society:
1. The widest possible expansion of political rights and freedom according to the
foregoing demands.
2. A progressive income tax for state and municipality instead of all those   25
existing, especially in place of the indirect tax which burdens the people.
3. Unrestrained right of combination [i.e. to form trade unions].
4. Shortening of the working day according to the needs of society.
5. Abolition of child labour and all female labour injurious to health and
morality.   30
6. Protective laws for the life and health of the worker. Sanitary control of the
homes of the workers. Supervision of the mines, factories, workshops and hand
industries by an officer elected by the people. An effectual law of enforcement.
7. Regulation of prison labour.
8. Full autonomy in the management of all labourers' fraternal and mutual   35
benefit funds.

This programme was agreed at a convention held at Gotha in 1875 at which the two wings of
the labour movement, the supporters of Lassalle and the supporters of Liebknecht, agreed to
join forces.

T. S. Hamerow, *The Age of Bismarck,* **pp. 230–2**

Questions

1 According to **2.9** and **2.10** what were the fundamental faults of capitalism?
2 How far were the long term goals outlined in the Gotha Programme
   [**2.11**] reflected in their specific demands?
3 Which of these demands would have been seen as reasonable by British
   or French governments in the last quarter of the nineteenth century?

2.12 Heinrich von Treitschke, *Socialism and its Sympathisers,* 1874

In this state of noble culture universal suffrage means organised indiscipline, it
amounts to a recognition of the revolt of sovereign ignorance, the revolt of the
soldier against the officer, of the journeyman against his master, of the worker

against his employer. But these destructive effects have already taken place to
excess and are no longer to be eliminated; to abolish the right would only   5
encourage the more the arrogance of the uncivilised. All we can do therefore, is
at least to protect the foundations of our monarchical state, the administration of
our localities and communities from the invasion of republican principles and to
protest against the assertion that the reward of ignorance is a result of
enlightened social policy ...   10

German Social Democracy really is 'as black' as it is painted in the majority of
cultured journals. It merits attention as a symptom of serious social abuses but it
does not offer us a single valid idea which would lend itself to discussion or
which could be absorbed into our social order. Envy and greed are the two
mighty forces that it employs to lift the old world from its hinges; it thrives on   15
the destruction of all ideals.

Treitschke was a celebrated German historian, also a member of the National Liberal
Party.

W. M. Simon, *Germany in the Age of Bismarck,* **p. 192**

2.13   Extracts from the Anti-Socialist Law of 21 October 1878

1. Organisations which through Social Democratic, Socialist, or Communist
activities, aim to overthrow the established state or social order are hereby
forbidden.

This same ban applies to organisations in which Social Democratic, Socialist or
Communist influence appears to be dedicated to the overthrow of the established   5
state or social order by breaching the public peace, or especially by endangering
class harmony ...

Such organisations include fraternities of all kinds ...

9. All meetings in which Social Democratic activities appear to be dedicated to
the overthrow of the established state or social order shall be dissolved.   10

Meetings, the activities of which justify the assumption that they are acting in
the sense prescribed in the first sentence of this law, are forbidden.

Such meetings include festivals and parades.

11. All publications in which Social Democratic, Socialist, or Communist
influence appears to be dedicated to the overthrow of the established state or   15
social order by breaching the public peace, or especially, by endangering class
harmony, are forbidden.

This ban on periodicals extends to all past issues, as soon as, on the basis of
this law, one single issue is forbidden.

16. The collection of contributions on demand by Social Democratic, Socialist or   20
Communist organisations for the purpose of overthrowing the established state or
social order, as well as public demands for contributions, are contrary to police
regulations. This ban will be made public.

17. Anyone who takes part as a member in a forbidden organisation, or anyone who exercises any activity in the interests of such an organisation, shall be   25
punished with a fine of up to 500 marks or with imprisonment of three months
... Those who take part in the work of such an organisation or its meetings as
chairman, leader, director, agent, speaker, or treasurer, or who call upon others to
attend meetings, will be sentenced to prison for a term of from one month to one   30
year ...

30. This law goes into effect on the day of its publication and remains in effect
until March 31, 1881

L. L. Snyder, *Documents of German History*, pp. **235–6**

Questions

1   On what grounds is Treitschke's indictment of German Social Democracy based [2.12]?
2   How widely do you think his views were shared by the German middle classes?
3   What explanation is given in **2.13** for the forbidding of Social Democrat, Socialist and Communist activities? Was there any justification for such a ban?

Bismarck's social policy

Bismarck's response to the threat presented by the Social Democrats was not wholly negative. Despite the fact that he makes no mention of them in his memoirs, perhaps the most constructive achievement of Bismarck's career were the laws passed in the 1880s to protect the German worker against the hazards of unregulated economic life. Bismarck's motives have been much questioned. He himself generally stressed the concern that a Christian states-man ought to feel for the poor, but equally he made no secret of his wish to steal the thunder of the Social Democrats and thus to lessen their appeal [2.14]. His critics and opponents, many of whom were in the Centre and Progressive Parties, saw a more Machiavellian purpose and accused him of using his insurance schemes to extend the power of the state and to win the support of the working classes for his regime, at the expense of the Reichstag [2.15]. In 1880, having added to his responsibilities the Prussian Ministry of Commerce, Bismarck set up a National Economic Council for Prussia on which groups representing Commerce, Industry and Agriculture were to be represented. It met for the first time in January 1881, and Bismarck's inten-tion was to create an Imperial Federal Council on the same lines. It was the suspicion created by these moves that explains why Bismarck's first Accident Insurance Law, introduced in January 1881, was so heavily amended in committee that he decided to proceed with it no further. Two features eliminated by the committee were an Imperial Insurance Institute and a contribution from the Reich government both of which would have strengthened links between the worker and the state. After a general election which resulted in gains by Bismarck's opponents, a much modified programme was introduced under which responsibility for various forms of insurance was much more widely dispersed between local authorities, employers' organisations, workers' co-operatives and the state.

In its final form Bismarck's social legislation contained three main elements. In 1883 a Sickness Insurance Law was passed providing payments to those off work through illness, and some assistance with medical care. The scheme was to be financed by employees and employers in the ratio of 2:1. In 1884 a revised Accident Insurance Law was passed, all payments now being provided by the employers without any contribution from the state. In 1889 Old Age Pensions and Invalidity Benefit were introduced, payable out of a fund to which employees, employers and the state all contributed. Thus, despite the suspicion which had greeted Bismarck's first initiative in 1881, by the end of the decade Germany had the most advanced system of social security in the world, and a prototype for others to copy, notably England. Sceptics have pointed out that these measures did nothing to halt the growth of the Social Democratic Party, and were in their early years limited in their impact. In 1885 Sickness and Health Insurance covered only 10% of the population. They still need to be taken into account when assessing Bismarck's record.

2.14   The motives behind Bismarck's social policies

2.14(a)   Bismarck in conversation with Moritz Busch, 26 June 1881

Anybody who has before him the prospect of a pension, be it ever so small, in old age or infirmity is much happier and more content with his lot, much more tractable and easy to manage, than he whose future is uncertain ... As the least taxed people in Europe we can bear with a good deal in that direction; and if the result enables us to secure the future of our operatives – uncertainty respecting which is the chief cause of their hatred of the state – the money will be well invested, for by spending it thus we may avert a social revolution which may break out fifty years hence, or ten and which, however short a time it lasts, will assuredly swallow up infinitely larger sums than those we now propose to expend ...   5

    10

Why should the regular soldier, disabled by war, or the official, have a right to be pensioned in his old age, and not the soldier of labour? This thing will make its own way; it has a future. When I die, possibly our policy will come to grief. But state socialism will have its day; and he who shall take it up again will assuredly be the man at the wheel.

Busch was a writer and journalist. At one time he was Bismarck's press secretary. Wehler describes him as 'his lackey'.

T. S. Hamerow, *The Age of Bismarck*, pp. 257–9

2.14(b) Bismarck's speech to the Reichstag at the introduction of the first Accident Insurance Bill, 2 April 1881

I am therefore of the opinion that a state which is at war with the infernal elements recently described to you here in detail, and which possesses among its citizens an overwhelming majority of sincere adherents of the Christian religion, should do for the poor, the weak and the old much more than this bill demands – as much as I hope to be able to ask of you next year. And such a state, especially 5 when it wishes to demonstrate its practical Christianity, should not refuse our own demands, for its own sake and for the sake of the poor!

T. S. Hamerow, *The Age of Bismarck*, p. 262

2.14(c) Speech by Bismarck on the second Accident Insurance Bill, 20 March 1884

The worker's real grievance is the uncertainty of his existence. He is not certain that he will always have work; he is not certain that he will always be healthy and he foresees that one day he will grow old and become incapable of work. Should he fall prey to poverty through a long illness then he is completely powerless on his own and society until now has recognised no obligation beyond the ordinary 5 duty of poor relief however faithfully and diligently he has worked. But ordinary poor relief leaves much to be desired, especially in the large towns where it is a great deal worse than in the countryside. If we read in the Berlin newspapers of suicides because of worries about food, of people dying directly from hunger and hanging themselves because they have nothing to eat, of people who announce in 10 the newspapers that they are homeless and have no accommodation, these are things which we from the country neither know nor understand. There the magistrate and the police would appear and restore the evicted and help provide the hungry with food and drink. Worries over subsistence are thus inconceivable. Now it appears that the local authorities responsible for Berlin do not act with 15 the same promptness as in the provinces. Meanwhile the fact remains that for a worker to succumb to poverty and dependence on poor relief in a large town is synonymous with misery, and this uncertainty makes him hostile and suspicious

towards society. Humanly speaking, this is not unnatural and so long as the state
does not take action, so long as the worker has no faith in the state's approaches   20
towards him, so long as his trust in the sincerity of the state has been
undermined by his suspicion of the government, then he will keep running for
help to where he can find it, as always to the socialist miracle doctor, and without
a second thought will accept his promises which cannot be fulfilled. Therefore I
believe that the Accident Insurance Bill with which we are proceeding will soften   25
the anxiety and hostility of the working classes. This will happen as soon as the
bill is fully implemented throughout agriculture, throughout the construction
industry and throughout all industrial undertakings, as we intend it to be.

The illness is not fully curable, but by suppressing the symptoms through
punitive legislation we shall only arrest it and force it inwards. I cannot embark   30
on that course only.

H. Rothfels, *Bismarck und der Staat*, pp. 375–6†

2.15   Bismarck's critics:

2.15(a)   Ludwig Bamberger, a member of the Progressive Party, in the debate on the Accident Insurance Bill, April 1881

After questioning the apparently generous motives behind the bill, Bamberger
suggested: 'the poor man must be shown that the state does not just exist for the
rich but also for him; he must be shown this positively, by gifts of money ...
Gentlemen is this a modern idea? ... That is the way ... the Roman Republic
thought in its decline ... This is no modern way of thinking, gentlemen, this is   5
not the state of the categorical imperative ... this is simply the state of the man
who goes about in a white toga in order to canvass votes and shake everybody by
the hand ... but not the state that is doing its duty.'

L. Gall, *Bismarck*, vol. 2, p. 130

2.15(b)   Theodor Lohmann, a close associate of Bismarck's, comments, in a private letter, on Bismarck's second Accident Insurance Bill in October 1883

In itself accident insurance is of secondary importance to him, he says, his
primary concern is to make use of the corporate co-operative associations he feels
must gradually be implemented for all productive classes in order *to acquire a
basis for a future parliament* that shall replace or complement the Imperial Diet as
an essential contributory factor in the legislative process – be it even, if the worst   5
comes to the worst, through the medium of a *coup d'état*.

L. Gall, *Bismarck*, vol. 2, pp. 166–7

Questions

1 How far do **2.14(a)–(c)** concur in the reasons Bismarck advances for his social insurance schemes?
2 What evidence can you find in **2.14** that Bismarck had a genuine concern for the poor?
3 What validity would you attach to the criticisms of Bismarck's social policy made by Ludwig Bamberger and Theodor Lohmann **[2.15]**?

Bismarck and protection

For the first eight years of its history Imperial Germany pursued a policy of free trade. Existing tariffs were consistently reduced in line with the prevailing consensus in the National Liberal Party on whose support Bismarck relied. The financial crisis of 1873 and the depression which ensued shook confidence in the economic arguments for free trade and producers both in industry and agriculture began to campaign for protection against cheap imports. Two pressure groups emerged to articulate these demands: the Association of German Iron and Steel Producers (1873) and the Confederation of Fiscal and Economic Reformers (1876). By 1878 Bismarck had become a convert to their views. As with so many of his policies his motives were various. He had never been a doctrinaire believer in free trade and may genuinely have been persuaded of the case for tariffs **[2.16]**; but he also saw in the extension of tariffs a mechanism for increasing imperial revenues and thus reducing his dependence on the Reichstag and on the *Matrikularbeiträge* [financial contributions] from the individual states which were the only form of direct taxation permitted under the constitution. Some historians have also claimed that in 1878 Bismarck made a conscious decision to embark on a new political strategy, exchanging his reliance on the National Liberal Party in favour of economic interest groups such as the Ruhr industrialists and the East Prussian landowners, both of whom would benefit from the new tariffs **[2.17]**.

Certainly, the economic package presented to the Reichstag in April 1879 could lend itself to each of these interpretations. Tariffs were to be placed on iron and iron-based goods and on grain, timber and cattle. There were to be increases in the internal duties on tobacco, salt and luxury goods. But to secure the passage of these measures Bismarck was forced to make a significant concession. Having forfeited the support of the National Liberals, he had to win that of the Centre Party. Following a succession of meetings with Windhorst, arranged by Bismarck's banker, Bleichröder, Bismarck accepted the so-called Clausula Franckenstein (Franckenstein was the new Vice-

President of the Reichstag, and a member of the Centre Party) under which all revenues to be derived from the tobacco tax and customs duties in excess of 130 million marks would be passed on to the individual states. Bismarck gained his tariff increases, but his financial dependence on the Reichstag and the states was not significantly reduced. In this form Bismarck's tariff legislation was passed by a combination of Centre, Conservative and right wing National Liberal deputies on 12 July 1879. The French ambassador in Berlin, St Vallier, described it as 'one of the most substantial triumphs of his political career' (Stern, *Gold and Iron*, p. 207).

The economic and political consequences of Bismarck's tariff legislation have been much debated. The German iron and steel industry certainly prospered in the 1880s and 1890s, but this may have had as much to do with technological improvements as with protection. Grain production east of the Elbe continued to grow, but at the expense of other forms of agriculture. Politically, the new tariffs have generally been thought to have had more damaging consequences [2.17].

2.16   Bismarck's speech to the Reichstag, 2 May 1879, urging the need for tariffs

In all questions such as these, I have regarded scientific theories with the same doubt with which I view the theories applied to other organic formations. Medical science, as compared with anatomy, has made but little progress in the last two thousand years with regard to those parts of the body that the eye cannot reach; today the riddle of organic changes in the body is as great as it was years   5
ago. It is the same thing when we consider the organism of the state. I am left completely cold by the dicta of abstract science. I make my judgments on the basis of practical experience of the time in which we are living. I see that those countries which have adopted protection are prospering, and that those countries which have free trade are deteriorating. Mighty England, that powerful athlete,   10
after she had strengthened her muscles, stepped out into the open market and said: 'Who will fight me? I am prepared to meet anybody.' Yet England herself is preparing to return slowly to protection, and in a few years, she will do it to save herself at least the home market.

In my opinion, since we have placed our tariffs at too low a rate (and I blame   15
myself for that, too), we have been slowly bleeding to death because of insufficient protection ... My personal request, and a most urgent one, is that we drop all questions of political parties in the face of this matter of general importance to all Germans.

L. L. Snyder, *Documents of German History*, pp. 240–41

2.17   The political effects of protection

2.17(a)

Moreover, it was both a cause and a consequence of this move towards
protectionism that party politics became ever more a question of *Interessenpolitik*,
of bargaining and manoeuvring for solid political advantages for those economic
interest groups which supported the various circles of political representatives. In
this situation, the Conservatives representing agriculture, the Free Conservatives   5
with their ties to heavy industry, the Centre, and even the SPD, could operate
more efficaciously than *laissez faire* liberals. An emphasis upon 'deals' rather than
principles also increased the political weight of that arch-bargainer, Bismarck, and
produced a further obstacle in the way of any progress towards parliamentarism
and democracy, which in any case were likely to be casualties in a time of severe   10
depression unless carefully nurtured.

P. M. Kennedy, *The Rise of Anglo-German Antagonism, 1860–1914* **p. 50**

2.17(b)

Judged from a purely economic standpoint, the whole policy of tariff protection
appeared dubious. It proved completely ineffective when faced with new
downturns in the economy after 1882 and 1890. In fact, as the highly-
recommended panacea of earlier policies intended to combat the business cycle, it
failed completely. But as a means of stabilising the political system, which was   5
where its real significance lay, it did perform a vitally important function. If, as
Gerschenkron has suggested, there was 'a great democratic opportunity' after
1876 to wrest political power from the pre-industrial *Junker* elite because of the
agrarian crisis, this chance was lost on account of an entire package of
government-inspired protectionist measures, of which the tariffs of 1879, 1885   10
and 1887 were only the most obvious. These tariffs won the support of industry,
which was itself seeking protection, and were agreed to by the representatives of
the bourgeoisie from their own motives of self-interest.

H-U. Wehler, *The German Empire,* **p. 38**

Questions

1   What arguments could Bismarck find to justify protection [2.16]?
2   How far do you think that the interpretations placed upon Bismarck's
    motives in **2.17(a)** and **(b)** are justified?
3   How significant was the adoption of protection in 1879 for the develop-
    ment of German politics?

3 Bismarck's foreign policy, 1871–90

By comparison with Bismarck's years in office between 1862 and 1871, when Prussia had fought three wars, during his years as imperial chancellor from 1871–90 Germany was dormant and Europe was at peace. This contrast raises two questions: how far was the more peaceful course pursued by Germany between 1871 and 1890 due to Bismarck's restraint, and how much credit should go to Bismarck for the peaceful resolution of conflicts in the Near East and in the wider arena of Africa and the Pacific where European rivalries clashed?

In examining Bismarck's foreign policy this chapter will focus particularly on these two issues. It has been claimed that, in contrast to his domestic policy, after 1871 Bismarck in international affairs was a force for stability: 'Convinced that his government had little to gain and much to lose in a new armed struggle, he laboured unceasingly to maintain harmony among the Great Powers' (Hamerow, *The Age of Bismarck*, p. 264). Others have been less charitable, seeing in his policy towards France and England, in particular, the subordination of good relations with these countries to the demands of internal politics; in the elaborate system of alliances he constructed, some of them mutually contradictory, an excessively complex legacy for his successors; and in the harnessing of Germany to Austria in the Dual Alliance of 1879, one of the fatal steps that led to the First World War.

The Europe Bismarck faced in 1871 was dominated by five major powers: a hostile and embittered France to the west of Germany, eager to recover the lost provinces of Alsace-Lorraine; a huge and rapidly industrialising Russia to the east, ready to support her co-religionists in the Balkans and anxious to secure control of the Dardanelles which linked the Black Sea to the Mediterranean; a Britain actively competing with Germany for world markets and at the peak of her imperial power; and an Austria, potentially friendly despite the war of 1866, but vulnerable to internal strains and tensions; finally, Germany herself, a newcomer on the international scene and regarded for that reason, and because of the warlike process by which she had arrived there, with initial suspicion and disquiet. There were potential sources of conflict in the Near East, where the Turkish empire was close to collapse; in Africa, where nine-tenths of the continent was partitioned between 1870 and 1890; in the Far East, where the race was on for naval bases and trading stations; and in Europe itself, where Franco-German hostility was never far below the surface.

Thus it was a potentially explosive world that Bismarck had to face. In the next twenty years he negotiated and intrigued, signed pacts and alliances, chaired European Conferences and played such a leading role in European diplomacy that Berlin became the nerve centre of Europe. At the same time Germany acquired a colonial empire five times the size of the European homeland and a formidable army. Before examining Bismarck's policies in detail, it would be as well to identify the main landmarks in these changes. The first significant development was the formation of the *Dreikaiserbund* (the Three Emperors' League) in 1873 through the Three Emperors' Agreement signed by the rulers of Austria, Germany and Russia [**3.12**]. It was severely threatened by a war scare with France in 1875, and by the Near East crisis that broke out in 1875 and was resolved, temporarily, at the Congress of Berlin in 1878. In 1879, for reasons that will be examined, Bismarck committed Germany to a full-scale military alliance with Austria, but this did not prevent a renewal of the *Dreikaiserbund* in 1881. In the following year the Dual Alliance was transformed into the Triple Alliance by the accession of Italy. In 1884–5 Bismarck embarked upon an active colonial policy for the first time, and Berlin once again hosted a conference, this time on the partition of West Africa, lasting from November 1884 to February 1885. In 1885 the Near East again became the focus of European attention as the Bulgarian question re-surfaced. It spluttered on until 1888. Bismarck's final years in office were marked by another war scare with France in 1887 which led to a major increase in defence spending, an attempt on Bismarck's part to strengthen Germany's ties with Italy, and a final effort to keep open the line to St Petersburg with the aptly named Reinsurance Treaty, signed in 1887. The passages which follow have been selected to illustrate Bismarck's overall policy aims [**3.1–3.3**]; relations with France; [**3.4–3.7**]; Bismarck's role as an honest broker in the Near East crisis [**3.8–3.11**]; the network of alliances and agreements negotiated by Bismarck between 1873 and 1887 [**3.12–3.17**]; and finally Bismarck's colonial policies [**3.18–3.21**].

The principles of Bismarck's foreign policy

Whether Bismarck was a pragmatic politician, trimming his policies according to the needs of the moment, or a statesman steering towards fixed objectives, has been much debated. He once said of himself: 'If I try to go through life with fixed principles I feel as though I am having to go along a narrow forest path with a large stick in my mouth' (Rothfels, *Bismarck und der Staat*, p. xix). The following passages illustrate his predicament. The first is taken from a speech made to the Reichstag in 1881, in which he stresses his objectives for Germany and his devotion to the national interest. The second is part of the so-called Kissingen Dictate, a note dictated by Bismarck to his son Herbert while on holiday at the Spa town of Bad Kissingen in 1877 in the middle of the Near East crisis. The third is an excerpt from a letter sent to the British prime minister, Lord Salisbury, in 1887, in which Bismarck spells out his hopes and fears. Each document is addressed to a different audience for a specific purpose, and this should be borne in mind.

3.1 Bismarck's speech to the Reichstag, 24 February 1881

For me there has only been a single compass, a single pole star by which I have steered: *Salus publica*! [the public good]. From the outset of my career, though acting at times perhaps rashly and unthinkingly, whenever I had the time to think about it, I always asked myself the question: 'What is most useful, what is most effective, what is the right policy for the Fatherland, for my dynasty, so long as I   5
am serving only Prussia, and today what is right for Germany?' ... One can act in different ways. There are many paths to Rome. There are times to rule with a light hand, there are times to be dictatorial. The situation is always changing. Nothing lasts for ever. But now the German empire is built and the German people united I insist that it stays firm and free of storms and is not merely   10
temporarily fortified on some of its sides; from its very beginning I have devoted my whole political career to its creation and consolidation. If you show me a single moment when I have not steered by this compass direction, then you can perhaps prove to me that I have erred, but you cannot prove that I have lost sight of the nation's goal for a single moment.

H. Rothfels, *Bismarck und der Staat*, p. 70†

3.2 An extract from the Kissingen Dictate, 15 June 1877

A French newspaper said of me recently that I had 'a coalition nightmare'. This kind of nightmare will long (and perhaps always) be a legitimate one for a German minister. Coalitions can be formed against us, based on the western powers with the addition of Austria, even more dangerous perhaps on a Russo-

Austrian-French basis; great intimacy between the two of the last-named powers   5
would always offer the third of them a means of exerting very effective pressure
on us. In our anxiety about these eventualities, I would regard as desirable results
of the eastern crisis (not immediately, but in the course of years): 1. gravitation of
Russian and Austrian interests and mutual rivalries towards the East; 2. Russia to
be obliged to take up a strong defensive position in the East and on its coasts,   10
and to need our alliance; 3. for England and Russia a satisfactory status quo,
which would give them the same interests in keeping what they hold as we have;
4. separation of England, on account of Egypt and the Mediterranean, from
France, which remains hostile to us; 5. relations between Russia and Austria
which would make it difficult for them to launch against us the anti-German   15
conspiracy to which centralist or clerical elements in Austria might be somewhat
inclined.

If I were able to work [Bismarck was absent from Berlin on one of his long
periods of recuperation at the time], I could complete and elaborate in detail the
picture I have in mind: not one of gaining territory, but of a political situation as   20
a whole, in which all the powers except France had need of us, and could thus be
deterred as far as possible from coalitions against us by their relations with each
other.

W. N. Medlicott and D. K. Coveney, *Bismarck and Europe*, pp. 102–3

3.3   A private letter from Bismarck to the English prime minister, Lord Salisbury, 22 November 1887

It would not be reasonable to accept that the government of a country of 50
million inhabitants – considering the degree of civilisation and the force of public
opinion present in Germany – could inflict on this country the sufferings which
accompany and follow every great war, victorious or not, without furnishing the
nation with sufficiently serious and clear reasons to convince public opinion of   5
the need for such a war. With an army like ours, recruited indifferently from all
classes in the population, representing the totality of active forces in the country
– with such an army the wars of the past, resulting from dynastic antipathies or
ambitions, could not occur. For nearly a quarter of a century Germany has
recruited 150,000 soldiers, so that today it has the power to dispose of 3–4   10
million men aged from 20 to 45, and trained for military service ...

These millions of men would flock to the colours and take up arms as soon as
a serious war threatened our national independence and the integrity of the
Empire. But this great war machine is too formidable, even in a country as
imbued with monarchical sentiment as ours, to be arbitrarily set in motion simply   15
by the royal will; on the contrary, the princes and peoples of the Empire would
have to be united in the conviction that the country, its independence and
recently achieved unity were in danger for these great levies of men to be raised
without danger. It follows that our military force is in the first place a defensive
weapon, destined only to be used when the nation is convinced that it must act to   20

repel aggression. Germany has little aptitude for fighting anything but a defensive war ...

[Bismarck then brings out the threats posed by Russia and France and the dangers of a simultaneous conflict against 'our two powerful neighbours', and hence the need to safeguard the existence of Austria as a great power. He concludes:]   25

From this point of view German policy will always be obliged to enter the line of battle if the independence of Austria is threatened or if England or Italy risk being invaded by French armies. German policy thus proceeds along a road necessarily prescribed by the political situation in Europe and from which it cannot be diverted by the antipathies or sympathies of either a monarch or a responsible minister.   30

H. Rothfels, *Bismarck und der Staat*, pp. 148–51†

Questions

1 Summarise the goals Bismarck claims to have pursued in **3.1**.
2 Why did Bismarck endure 'a coalition nightmare' [**3.2, line 1**], and were his fears justified?
3 In the light of **3.2** and **3.3** did Bismarck see Germany as a satiated power after 1871?
4 How far do all these passages suggest that after 1871 Bismarck's primary goal was the security rather than extension of the Reich?

Bismarck's policies towards France

Bismarck's policies towards France were vitiated from the start by his decision to annex Alsace-Lorraine, a decision which, while he might have regretted in private, he never showed the least inclination to reverse in public. It is also arguable that he made Franco-German relations worse than they need have been by deliberately exaggerating the dangers of a French war of revenge, notably in 1875 and 1887. Each crisis was provoked by a French initiative, but Bismarck's response was out of all proportion, it might seem, to the threat. In 1875 German military leaders, notably Moltke, took an administrative change in the French army under which regiments were now to have four battalions rather than three as heralding an increase in the fighting strength of the French army by 144,000 men. Bismarck was similarly disturbed by an order for 10,000 horses from Holstein [**3.4**]. Two inflammatory articles appeared in the German press, one in the *Kölnische Zeitung* on 5 April and another, headed 'Is War in Sight?', in the *Berliner Post* on 9 April. Whether or not Bismarck inspired these articles has never been finally established [3.5]. It soon became clear that Bismarck had overreached himself. Britain and Russia offered their support for France and the war scare evaporated.

Thereafter, Bismarck adopted a more conciliatory stance towards France, positively encouraging her colonial ambitions in North Africa and Indo-China in the 1880s, and urging the French ambassador, Courcel, in 1884 to 'forgive Sedan as after 1815 [they had learned] to forgive Waterloo' (Craig, *Germany, 1866–1945*, p. 124). But in 1886–7 Bismarck exploited another war scare to secure an electoral victory and increase his control over arms expenditure. The war scare arose out of the militant language employed by General Boulanger, the French war minister appointed in 1886, and his supporters. In November 1886 Bismarck introduced a bill into the Reichstag renewing the Septennate (the seven year military budget) one year before the old one was due to expire, and increasing military spending by 10%, a further 40,000 men in the army's peace time strength. The bill was defeated by a coalition of Liberals, Social Democrats and Centre Party deputies by 186 votes to 154. The Reichstag was dissolved and in the ensuing election campaign Bismarck again raised the spectre of French aggression [3.6]. His tactics paid off. His conservative and patriotic supporters won a handsome victory in the February election and the Army Bill went through by 233 votes to 40. Whether Bismarck really believed in the danger of a war is highly unlikely, as the difference between his public and private pronouncements indicate. It was the impression that counted, and in this light it is hardly surprising that Franco-German relations in 1890 were little better than they had been in 1871.

3.4   The war scare of 1875: Bismarck writes to the German ambassador, Hohenlohe, in Paris, 26 February 1875

On the departure of the courier I learn that German horse-dealers have been commissioned to buy up forthwith for France 10,000 saddle horses with no restriction on price, with 50fr. provisions for each. Even if the measure is only the natural result of the agreed reorganization, nevertheless we have no reason to aid and abet a reorganization which bears the stamp of a preparation for war, by   5 supplying German horses. It therefore seems imperative to take counter-measures.

W. N. Medlicott and D. K. Coveney, *Bismarck and Europe,* **p. 88**

3.5   An entry from the diary of Ludwig Bamberger, National Liberal deputy in the Reichstag, 19 June 1875

When on April 10 I arrived in Berlin from Paris, suddenly a rumour of war had broken out. Two semi-official articles in the 'Post' and in the 'Kölnische Zeitung' had launched it, particularly the one in the 'Post' under the headline: 'Is war in sight?' ...What was Bismarck's purpose in this? Even today, when everything has been denied and soothed away, nobody knows. All that people seem to agree on   5 is that Bismarck wanted the rumour and undoubtedly instigated it.

W. M. Simon, *Germany in the Age of Bismarck*, p. 89

3.6   Bismarck's speech to the Reichstag in defence of the Army Bill, 11 January 1887

The possibility of a French attack, which today is not imminent, will recur as soon as France thinks she is stronger than we are, either by alliances or by being better armed. In case of an unsuccessful war, the peace of 1870 would be mere child's play as compared with the peace of 1890. We should have the same French against us who we met from 1807 to 1813, and who for years would again   5 suck our blood so that we should be paralysed for thirty years.

C. Grant Robertson, *Bismarck*, p. 443

3.7   Bismarck's policies in the election campaign of 1887

An additional factor [in explaining the success of Bismarck's supporters] was that before the election Bismarck had irresponsibly had the atmosphere of crisis heightened not only at home but with respect to foreign policy. Twelve years previously, at the time of the 'War in Sight' crisis, the connections had been less clear. Now, with a fresh incendiary article by Constantin Rossler appearing in the   5 Berlin *Post* on 31 January 1887 under the title '*Auf des Messers Schneide*' ('The Razor's Edge'), they were quite unequivocal. The call-up of 72,000 reservists for exercises with a new repeating gun in Alsace-Lorraine at the beginning of February, the orchestrated rumours about a projected war loan in the sum of no less than 300 million marks, which sowed panic on both the Paris and the Berlin   10 stock exchanges – all these things served to conjure up, to the advantage of the 'parties of order', a danger in which Bismarck did not seriously believe or that at any rate he regarded as far inferior to that of an entanglement in the east; unless Boulanger came to power he told friends around this time, war was 'completely out of the question'.

L. Gall, *Bismarck*, vol. 2, p. 190

Questions

1. How far do **3.4** and **3.5** support the view that Bismarck deliberately encouraged the war scare with France in 1875?
2. In the light of **3.7** how genuine were the fears of France expressed by Bismarck in **3.6**?
3. How do you account for the evident inconsistencies in Bismarck's attitude to France between 1871 and 1887?

Bismarck and the Near East

If Bismarck's policy towards France can hardly be described as conciliatory, during the Near East crises of 1875–8 and 1885–7 he was much more circumspect. Whether he was also the constructive statesman that has sometimes been claimed is open to question.

The first crisis erupted in May 1875 with a revolt by Bosnian Slavs against their Turkish rulers, posing for the first time the dilemma that would haunt the powers in the Balkan Peninsula for the next forty years: 'Once the Balkan Slavs were astir, no Russian government dared let them fail; Austria-Hungary dared not let them succeed' (A. J. P. Taylor, *The Struggle for Mastery in Europe*, p. 229). On this occasion both powers managed to secure sufficient benefits from the crisis, at the expense of the Turkish empire, to postpone a collision. Various efforts were made to contain the crisis by compelling the Turks to treat their nominally Christian subjects better, in particular the Andrassy Note of 30 December 1875 and the Berlin Memorandum of 13 May 1876. Both failed to command universal support; on 29 May 1876 the sultan abdicated; in June the revolt spread to Bulgaria and war was declared on the Turks by Serbia and Montenegro. On 8 July Andrassy, the Austrian foreign minister, met his Russian counterpart, Gorchakov, at Reichstadt where a verbal agreement was reached under which in the event of Turkey's defeat Austria would have the right to occupy Bosnia, while Russia would recover the part of Bessarabia she had lost after the Crimean War.

Turkish success in crushing the Bulgarian revolt and the cruel way in which it was done (the Bulgarian massacres which so outraged Gladstone) finally provoked Russia into declaring war on Turkey on 24 April 1877. The Russian advance was unexpectedly held up at Plevna, and Russian armies did not reach the outskirts of Constantinople until December. There they halted and imposed on the Turks the treaty of San Stefano (3 March 1878) whose prime feature was the creation of a large and independent Bulgaria.

This would become, so it was anticipated, a buffer state under Russian domination. This was more than Austria or Britain were prepared to accept. After threats from Britain, notably the despatch of Indian troops to Malta, an agreement was reached on 30 May between Lord Salisbury, British foreign secretary, and Shuvalov, the Russian ambassador in London, to partition Bulgaria. This was followed on 6 June by an agreement between Britain and Austria under which British support for the Austrian claim to Bosnia secured Austrian backing for the smaller Bulgaria wanted by Britain. These agreements were already in place before the Congress of Berlin convened under Bismarck's chairmanship on 13 June.

Bismarck's purpose throughout the crisis was to avoid committing himself either to Austria or to Russia, while trying also to ensure that the existing power balance in Europe was not seriously upset [3.8]. Whether he actively sought the role of 'honest broker' is less certain [3.8d] but his performance in that role is generally held to have been successful. Throughout the twenty sessions he evidently dominated the proceedings [3.9], and secured the compliance of all the interested parties to the uneasy compromises which marked the Treaty of Berlin [3.10].

3.8   Bismarck's policy during the Near East crisis

3.8(a)   Letter to Bernhard von Bülow (the elder), secretary of state for foreign affairs, 14 August 1876

The Three Emperors' Alliance has so far been a guarantee of peace; if it is weakened and broken because of the elective affinities of Austria and England or Russia and France, the incompatibility of Austro-Anglo-Russian interests in the East will lead to war ... Day after day Germany would be called upon to be the arbitrator between the two hostile groups of the Congress, the most thankless task   5
that can fall to our lot; and as we are not disposed, firmly and from the outset to attach ourselves to one of the two groups, the prospect is that our three friends, Russia, Austria and England will leave the Congress with ill feeling towards us because none of them has had the support from us that he expected.

W. N. Medlicott and D. K. Coveney, *Bismarck and Europe*, p. 97

3.8(b)   Dictate of 14 October 1876 by Bismarck

The more acute the situation becomes, the more clearly, in my opinion, we must remember and in our diplomatic dealings give expression to the fact that our main interest lies not in this, or that or the other arrangement of the circumstances of the Turkish Empire but in the position in which the powers friendly to us are placed with regard to ourselves and one another. The question   5 of whether, as a result of the Eastern troubles, we end up on permanently bad terms with Britain, even more with Austria, but most of all with Russia, is of infinitely greater importance for the future of Germany than all Turkey's relations with its subjects and the European powers.

L. Gall, *Bismarck*, vol. 2, pp. 49–50

3.8(c)   Bismarck's speech to the Reichstag, 5 December 1876

In Turkey we have the interests, which I have already explained, of general sympathy with our fellow Christians, and if the previous speaker quoted a report that he himself treats as apocryphal, that I am supposed to have said that in the whole of the Orient there is no interest that is worth the revenues of a single Pomeranian manor, that is wrong. In all such legends there is a grain of truth,   5
and always a bit of falsehood too. (Much laughter.) What I said was: I will not advise active participation of Germany in these things as long as I see no interest for Germany in it which – forgive the blunt expression – would be worth the healthy bones of a single Pomeranian musketeer. I have sought to emphasize that we must be more sparing with the blood of our people and our soldiers when it is   10
a question of deliberately embarking on a policy in which no interest of ours is involved.

W. N. Medlicott and D. K. Coveney, *Bismarck and Europe*, pp. 99–100

3.8(d)   Bismarck's speech to the Reichstag, 19 February 1878

Play the German card, throw it on the table – and everyone will know what measures to take or how to circumvent it. That is not practical if we are to negotiate peace. I do not conceive peace negotiations as a situation in which, faced by divergent views, we play the arbitrator and say: It shall be thus, and it is backed by the might of the German empire (very good!), but I imagine a more   5
modest role, indeed – I do not hesitate to quote you something from everyday life – more that of an honest broker, who really intends to do business. (Laughter.)

W. N. Medlicott and D. K. Coveney, *Bismarck and Europe*, pp. 103–4

3.9   Bismarck's chairmanship of the Congress of Berlin

The Congress was a show-piece for Bismarck's personality. It was the only international gathering over which he presided; and no one ever presided in the same manner. He gave the great statesmen of Europe a taste of the rough jovial manner with which he entertained German politicians at his 'beer evenings' ... He bustled through the formal sessions commenting audibly if the Turkish delegate   5
or even Lord Salisbury dared to raise a new point ... Protocol was ignored; everything subordinated to punctual and enormous meals. Bismarck was to be

seen stuffing shrimps into his mouth with one hand, cherries with the other and
insisting – not surprisingly – that he must leave soon for a cure at Kissingen.
Any real difficulty was settled by Bismarck privately behind the scenes. But the   10
Congress was a model for all time in its way of doing business and reaching
results, even if less in the results themselves. Bismarck was not interested in these
or in the fate of 'the people down there'. 'We are not here to consider the
happiness of the Bulgarians but to secure the peace of Europe'.

A. J. P. Taylor, *Bismarck*, pp. 176–7

3.10   The Treaty of Berlin, 1878 (selected terms)

ARTICLE 1. Bulgaria is constituted an autonomous and tributary principality
under the suzerainty of His Imperial Majesty the Sultan; it will have a Christian
government and a national militia. The Prince of Bulgaria shall be freely elected
by the population and confirmed by the Sublime Porte [the Turkish Empire],
with the assent of the Powers. No member of the reigning dynasties of the Great   5
European Powers may be elected Prince of Bulgaria ...

ARTICLE 13. A province is formed south of the Balkans which will take the
name of 'Eastern Rumelia', and will remain under the direct political and military
authority of His Imperial Majesty the Sultan, under conditions of administrative
autonomy. It shall have a Christian Governor-General ...   10

ARTICLE 25. The Provinces of Bosnia and Herzegovina shall be occupied and
administered by Austria-Hungary ...

ARTICLE 26. The independence of Montenegro is recognized by the Sublime
Porte and by all those High Contracting Parties who have not hitherto admitted it.

ARTICLE 32. The High Contracting Parties recognize the independence of the   15
Principality of Serbia ...

ARTICLE 43. The High Contracting Parties recognize the independence of
Rumania ...

L. L. Snyder, *Documents of German History*, pp. 237–8

Questions

1   From the evidence of **3.8(a)–(c)** how did Bismarck perceive German
    interests in the Near East crisis?
2   How far did Bismarck's chairmanship of the Berlin Congress [**3.9**] fulfil
    the role of 'honest broker' which he had envisaged [**3.8(d)**]?
3   With what justification could Russia feel that her interests had been sub-
    ordinated to those of Austria in the Treaty of Berlin [**3.10**]?

3.11   The Balkans 1878–81

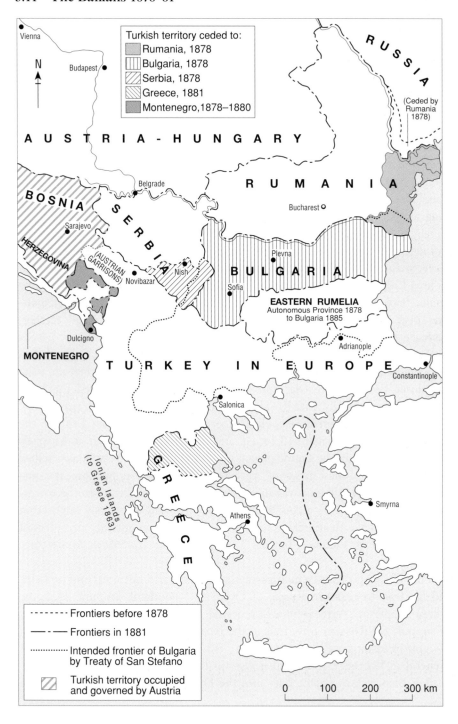

Turkish territory ceded to:
- Rumania, 1878
- Bulgaria, 1878
- Serbia, 1878
- Greece, 1881
- Montenegro, 1878–1880

Vienna

N

Budapest

RUSSIA

(Ceded by Rumania 1878)

AUSTRIA-HUNGARY

BOSNIA

Belgrade

RUMANIA

Bucharest

HERZEGOVINA

Sarajevo

SERBIA

(AUSTRIAN GARRISONS)

Novibazar

Nish

Plevna

BULGARIA

Sofia

EASTERN RUMELIA
Autonomous Province 1878
to Bulgaria 1885

Dulcigno

MONTENEGRO

TURKEY   IN   EUROPE

Adrianople

Constantinople

Salonica

Ionian Islands
(to Greece 1863)

GREECE

Athens

Smyrna

- - - - - - - Frontiers before 1878

— · — Frontiers in 1881

· · · · · · · · · · · · Intended frontier of Bulgaria
by Treaty of San Stefano

Turkish territory occupied
and governed by Austria

0   100   200   300 km

Bismarck's alliance system

Germany's position at the centre of Europe, surrounded by potentially or in the case of France certainly hostile neighbours, made her peculiarly vulnerable, or so Bismarck evidently believed. Between 1873 and 1887 he bound Germany into a series of pacts and alliances, some of them mutually contradictory, in his persistent search for security. But every alliance carried with it reciprocal obligations, and whether German or European security was actually enhanced by the links Bismarck forged remains an open question. What motives determined his choice of allies? He seems instinctively to have preferred the conservative monarchies of Austria and Russia to the parliamentary regimes of France and Britain. He also wanted, as he put it to the Russian ambassador in Berlin, Saburov, in 1880, 'to try to be one of three as long as the world is governed by an unstable equilibrium of five powers' (Craig, *Germany, 1866–1945*, p. 115). These considerations undoubtedly influenced him in making the *Dreikaiserabkommen* (Three Emperors' Agreement) in 1873, which was renewed in 1881 as the *Dreikaiserbund* (Three Emperors' League) [3.12]. Bismarck was finally forced into making a choice between his two conservative allies because of their mutual antagonism over the Balkans, but his commitment to Austria went further, perhaps, than it need have done.

Russian dissatisfaction with the outcome of the Congress of Berlin led to estrangement and disillusion with Germany. Bismarck came to feel the need for closer ties with Austria, and on 7 October 1879 he signed the Dual Alliance. Its primarily anti-Russian purpose is revealed in its terms [3.13]. There were other motives as well. Bismarck undoubtedly hoped to win the support of South Germans [3.14(a)], and he may have felt that as Austria's ally Germany would be better placed to restrain her than simply as a fellow member of the Three Emperors' Agreement. Whatever its purpose, the outcome of the Dual Alliance was to tie 'the trim Prussian frigate to the worm-eaten Austrian galleon', a course which Bismarck had vigorously opposed in 1854, and to make Bismarck's successors, so it has been argued, 'prisoners of the statesmen in Vienna' (Taylor, *The Struggle for Mastery in Europe*, pp. 262–5).

This was an outcome which Bismarck certainly did not want and he twice did his best to reassure Russia of Germany's goodwill. In June 1881 the Three Emperors' Agreement was renewed, this time with specific promises of support for Russian ambitions in the Near East [3.15]. On the other hand his apprehensions were aroused by a visit to Paris by a pan-Slav Russian General in February 1882, and it was this as much as anything which persuaded Bismarck to accept Italy into the Dual Alliance, which now became a Triple Alliance, in May 1882 [**3.16**]. If Germany could be sure of Italian support against France, this would free Austrian troops for action against Russia.

But Bismarck still hoped to remain on good terms with Russia. The incompatibility of Russian and Austrian aims in the Balkans was exposed again in the Bulgarian crisis which erupted in 1885. It was sparked off by a popular revolt in Eastern Rumelia, which now sought to unite with Bulgaria. Russia was unwilling to accept this outcome because she no longer trusted Prince Alexander of Battenberg, her protégé and ruler of Bulgaria. In September 1886 Alexander was deposed with Russian connivance, providing Russia with an excuse to intervene. Austria made clear her opposition to any such interference. These tensions persuaded Tsar Alexander III not to renew the Three Emperors' Agreement when it expired in June 1887. Bismarck, who had been considering a new treaty with Russia since January, began serious negotiations with the Russian ambassador in Berlin, Paul Shuvalov, and these were successfully concluded on 18 June 1887. The Reinsurance Treaty, as it came to be known, was an attempt on Bismarck's part to ensure Russian neutrality in the event of a war with France. The price was German acknowledgement of Russia's claims in the Balkans [**3.17**]. Needless to say the treaty was kept absolutely secret until Bismarck, in a fit of pique, revealed it publicly through an article in a Hamburg newspaper on 24 October 1896. By that date the treaty had long been a dead letter. It had not been renewed by Kaiser Wilhelm II in 1890. Its revelation was still a profound shock, especially to Austria. What is perhaps equally surprising is that shortly after the Treaty was signed, Bismarck supported the 'Lombard-Verbot' of 10 November 1887 under which the Reichsbank was forbidden to accept Russian securities as collateral for loans, thus discouraging any future German investment in Russia. This decision was announced one week before the visit of Alexander III to Berlin. It has been explained as an attempt 'to bully an opponent into friendship' (Stern, *Gold and Iron*, p. 442), as a warning against the increase in Russian agricultural exports and as an attempt to limit Russia's economic growth (Gall, *Bismarck*, vol. 2, p. 154). In any event, it sat awkwardly with the Reinsurance Treaty. **3.12**–**3.17** highlight the most important terms of these agreements and the reasoning behind the most crucial of them, the Dual Alliance.

3.12   The Three Emperors' Agreement 6 June, 22 October 1873

His Majesty the Emperor of Austria and King of Hungary and His Majesty the Emperor of all the Russias
Wishing to give a practical form to the thought governing their close entente,

With the aim of consolidating the peace which exists at the moment in Europe, and having their heart set on eliminating the chances of war which could disturb it,   5

Convinced that this aim could not be better attained than by a direct personal agreement between the rulers, an agreement independent of any changes which might occur in their administrations, have agreed upon the following points:

1. Their Majesties promise mutually, even though the interests of their country   10 might differ with respect to particular questions, to consult together so that these divergences do not take precedence over considerations of a higher order which may be preoccupying them. Their Majesties have decided to oppose any move to separate them with regard to principles which they consider themselves alone capable of assuring, and, if necessary, to impose the maintenance of peace in   15 Europe against all attempts to destroy it, from whatever quarter they come.

2. In the case of an attack coming from a third power threatening to compromise the peace of Europe Their Majesties are mutually bound to come to an agreement first among themselves, without seeking or contracting new alliances, in order to agree on the line of conduct they will follow in common.   20

[Articles 3 and 4 follow.]

Schönbrunn, 25 May/6 June 1873

The initial agreement was signed by Emperor Franz Josef of Austria and Tsar Alexander II of Russia on 6 June; Emperor Wilhelm I of Germany acceded to the agreement on 22 October.

W. N. Medlicott and D. K. Coveney, *Bismarck and Europe*, pp. 86–7

3.13   The Austro-German Treaty of Alliance, 7 October 1879

Article I. Should, contrary to their hope, and against the loyal desire of the two High Contracting Parties, one of the two Empires be attacked by Russia, the High Contracting Parties are bound to come to the assistance one of the other with the whole war strength of their Empires, and accordingly only to conclude peace together and upon mutual agreement.   5

Articles II. Should one of the High Contracting Parties be attacked by another Power, the other High Contracting Party binds itself hereby, not only not to support the aggressor against its High Ally, but to observe at least a benevolent neutral attitude towards its fellow Contracting Party.

Should, however, the attacking party in such a case be supported by Russia,   10 either by active co-operation or by military measures which constitute a menace to the Party attacked, then the obligation stipulated in Article I of this Treaty, for reciprocal assistance with the whole fighting force, becomes equally operative ...

Article III. The duration of this Treaty shall be provisionally fixed at five years from the day of ratification ...   15

Article IV. This Treaty shall, in conformity with its peaceful character, and to avoid any misinterpretation, be kept secret by the two High Contracting Parties ...

W. N. Medlicott and D. K. Coveney, *Bismarck and Europe*, pp. 117–8

3.14   Reasons for the Dual Alliance

3.14(a)   A letter from Bismarck to Wilhelm I, 31 August 1879

I already had the feeling at the peace negotiations in Nikolsburg in 1866 [ending the Austro-Prussian War], thinking about our thousand years of common German history, that we should sooner or later have to create a substitute for the tie that had then been broken in order that the German constitution be reformed.

L. Gall, *Bismarck*, vol. 2, p. 119

3.14(b)   Bismarck's Reflections and Reminiscences

In short, if in deciding between the Russian and the Austrian alliance I gave preference to the latter, it was not that I was in any degree blind to the perplexities which made the choice difficult. I regarded it as no less enjoined upon us to cultivate neighbourly relations with Russia after, than before, our defensive alliance with Austria; for perfect security against the disruption of the ⁵ chosen combination is not to be had by Germany, while it is possible for her to hold in check the anti-German fits and starts of Austro-Hungarian feeling so long as German policy maintains the bridge which leads to St Petersburg, and allows no chasm to intervene between us which cannot be spanned ...

It is, however, no part of the policy of the German Empire to lend her ¹⁰ subjects, to expend her blood and treasure, for the purpose of realizing the designs of a neighbour Power. In the interest of the European political equilibrium the maintenance of the Austro-Hungarian monarchy as a strong independent Great Power is for Germany an object for which she might in need stake her own power with a good conscience. But Vienna should abstain from ¹⁵ going outside this security, and deducing from the alliance claims which it was not concluded to support.

A. J. Butler, (ed.), *Otto von Bismarck*, vol. 2, pp. 272–4

3.15   The Three Emperors' League, 18 June 1881

Article I. In case one of the High Contracting Parties should find itself at war with a fourth Great Power, the two others shall maintain towards it a benevolent neutrality and shall devote their efforts to the localization of the conflict.

This stipulation shall apply likewise to a war between one of the three Powers and Turkey, but only in the case where a previous agreement shall have been   5
reached between the Three Courts as to the results of this war.

Article II. Russia, in agreement with Germany, declares her firm resolution to respect the interests arising from the new position assured to Austria-Hungary by the Treaty of Berlin ...

Article III. [The Three Courts recognize the obligatory closing of the Straits of   10
the Bosphorus and the Dardanelles to foreign warships agreed to at the Congress of Berlin.]

Article IV. This Treaty shall be in force during a period of three years, dating from the day of exchange of ratifications.

Article V. [Treaty and Protocol attached to be Secret.]   15

SEPARATE PROTOCOL TO THE THREE EMPERORS' LEAGUE

1. Bosnia and Herzegovina.
Austria-Hungary reserves the right to annex these provinces at whatever moment they shall judge opportune.
3. Eastern Rumelia.   20
The Three Powers oppose Turkish occupation of Eastern Rumelia or of the Balkans 'as full of peril for the general peace'.
4. Bulgaria.
The Three Powers will not oppose the eventual reunion of Bulgaria and Eastern Rumelia ...   25
5. Attitude of Agents in the East.
Representatives and agents of the three Courts to be instructed to 'smooth out their divergences by friendly explanations between themselves in each special case', and where they fail 'to refer matters to their Governments'.

W. N. Medlicott and D. K. Coveney, *Bismarck and Europe*, **pp. 126–8**

3.16   The Triple Alliance Treaty between Germany, Austria-Hungary and Italy, 20 May 1882

Article II. In case Italy, without provocation on her part, should be attacked by France, for any reason whatsoever, the two other Contracting Parties shall be bound to lend help and assistance with all their forces to the party attacked.

This same obligation shall devolve upon Italy in case of any aggression without direct provocation by France against Germany.   5

Article III. If one, or two, of the High Contracting Parties, without direct provocation on their part, should chance to be attacked and to be engaged in a

war with two or more Great Powers non signatory to the present Treaty, the
casus foederis will arise simultaneously for all the High Contracting Parties.

W. N. Medlicott and D. K. Coveney, *Bismarck and Europe*, p. 130

3.17 The Reinsurance Treaty, 18 June 1887

Article I. If one of the High Contracting Parties should find itself at war with a
third Great Power, the other would maintain a benevolent neutrality and would
try to localize the conflict. This provision would not apply to a war against
Austria or France resulting from an attack on one of these two Powers by one of
the High Contracting Parties.   5

Article II. Germany recognizes the rights historically acquired by Russia in the
Balkan peninsula and particularly the legitimacy of her preponderant and decisive
influence in Bulgaria and Eastern Rumelia ...

Article III. [Confirms closing of the Straits of the Bosphorus and of the
Dardanelles.]   10

Article IV. The present Treaty shall remain in force for the space of three years
from the day of exchange of ratifications.
[Articles V, VI – provisions relating to secrecy and ratification.]

ADDITIONAL AND VERY SECRET PROTOCOL, 18 JUNE 1887

In order to complete the stipulations of Articles II and III of the secret treaty   15
concluded on the same date, the two Courts are agreed on the following points:
1. Germany, as in the past, will lend Russia a free hand in order to re-establish a
regular and legal government in Bulgaria. – She promises not to give in any case
Her consent to the restoration of the Prince of Battenberg [Alexander].
2. If His Majesty the Emperor of Russia should find Himself under the necessity   20
of assuming the task of defending the entrance of the Black Sea in order to
safeguard the interests of Russia, Germany undertakes to accord Her benevolent
neutrality and Her moral and diplomatic support to the measures which His
Majesty may deem it necessary to take to guard the key of His Empire.

W. N. Medlicott and D. K. Coveney, *Bismarck and Europe*, pp. 163–4

Questions

1 What obligations did the Three Emperors' Agreement of 1873 [**3.12**] impose on its signatories?
2 In what ways did the Three Emperors' League of 1881 [**3.15**] alter the Treaty of Berlin [**3.10**]?
3 How far do **3.12** and **3.15** convey an accurate impression of where responsibility for the conduct of foreign policy actually lay in the countries concerned?
4 In what circumstances, under the terms of the Dual Alliance [**3.13**] were Germany and Austria committed to come to one another's support?
5 Compare the motives Bismarck gives for the Dual Alliance in **3.14(a)** and **(b)**.
6 What limitations does Bismarck try to place on the Dual Alliance [**3.14(b)**]?
7 Which loophole was left to Italy under the terms of the Triple Alliance [**3.16**] that enabled her to remain neutral in 1914?
8 Do you see any clear contradiction between the Dual Alliance [**3.13**] and the Reinsurance Treaty [**3.17**]?
9 What is the significance of the Very Secret Protocol attached to the Reinsurance Treaty [**3.17**]?

Bismarck's colonial policies

The final enigma to be examined in Bismarck's foreign policy is his attitude to colonisation. In a private conversation held in 1880 with Prince Chlodwig zu Hohenlohe-Schillingsfürst, later president of the Colonial League, Bismarck evidently denied any interest in colonies [**3.18**]. When nearly at the end of his career he made much the same disclaimer in a private conversation with Eugen Wolff, a colonial enthusiast [**3.19**]. Yet in 1884–5 he promoted and supported German claims to parts of South West, West and East Africa; he championed the interests of German traders in the Pacific; and he took the initiative in convening and himself chaired the West Africa Colonial Conference that met in Berlin in November 1884 to February 1885. Despite the strident demands for 'a place in the sun' made by Bülow when foreign secretary in 1897, it was in fact under Bismarck's direction that the bulk of the German empire was acquired.

Various motives have been ascribed to Bismarck to explain his apparent change of heart. He himself defended it in public as a response to popular pressures [3.20]. In private he almost certainly had a more Machiavellian purpose [3.21(a), (b)]. He was, it would seem, anxious to pick a quarrel with Britain as a way of reducing the Anglophile influence of the Crown Prince and his supporters, while using the colonial issue to drum up support for the 1884 Reichstag elections.

Long-term factors and immediate considerations also played their parts. In the 1880s the German economy was suffering from lack of markets and the same pressures that prompted the adoption of tariffs in 1879 led to a growing demand for colonial outlets. In 1882 the Colonial League was founded with this purpose in mind. Imperialism might also, it was hoped, prove a useful diversion to wean the workers from socialism. Another motive was to siphon off the huge flood of German emigrants (203,000 in 1882 alone) to areas where good German stock would not be lost to the empire.

It was, finally, the initiatives of particular groups and individuals that persuaded Bismarck to act. In 1883 F. A. E. Lüderitz, a Bremen tobacco merchant, established a trading station at Angra Pequena on the inhospitable coast of South West Africa. He sought Bismarck's protection, and after prolonged negotiations with the British government, who acted in a very dilatory way, Bismarck in April 1884 asserted German claims to that stretch of coast line. At the same time a Doctor Gustav Nachtigall was despatched to assert German claims to the Cameroons in West Africa. Britain, France, Portugal and Belgium all had interests in West Africa, too. Bismarck, fearing that German traders might be excluded from the Congo basin, convened the West Africa Conference that met in Berlin in November 1884. As in 1878, Bismarck dominated the proceedings. He defined the goals of the Conference as: free trade in the Congo basin; free navigation on the river Niger and agreement on the formalities for the future annexation of territory (T. Pakenham, *The Scramble for Africa*, p. 241). Though the Conference concerned itself mainly with defining the boundaries of the Congo Free State to be created by King Leopold of Belgium, it did reach agreement on the goals set out by Bismarck and in this respect he could claim to have once again played the role of honest broker. It did not prevent him from supporting the bid of Carl Peters, an impassioned believer in Germany's imperial destiny and founder of the Company for German Colonisation, to establish a protectorate in East Africa. Bismarck announced his approval of this venture on 3 March 1885, just a few days after the Berlin Conference had ended. He was similarly ready to support German claims in Fiji, New Guinea and Samoa. The following documents illustrate Bismarck's changing attitudes to colonisation and the reasoning behind them.

3.18   Bismarck in conversation with Prince Chlodwig zu Hohenlohe-Schillingsfürst, February 1880

The Chancellor refuses all talk of colonies. He says that we haven't an adequate fleet to protect them, and our bureaucracy is not skilful enough to direct the government of such territories.

W. N. Medlicott and D. K. Coveney, *Bismarck and Europe*, p. 138

3.19   Bismarck in conversation with Eugen Wolff, 5 December 1888

Your map of Africa is all very fine, but my map of Africa lies in Europe. Here is Russia and here – pointing to the left – is France, and we are in the middle; that is my map of Africa.

Wolff was a well known explorer and colonialist. He had just explained to Bismarck the current situation in Africa.

L. Gall, *Bismarck*, vol. 2, p. 143

3.20   Bismarck's speech to the Reichstag, 2 March 1885

We do not claim to direct the colonial ventures of the German people according to a bureaucratic formula and a particular system about which we have a clear view; but we intend to follow with the protection of the empire those ventures where we recognise a probability of development, and justification for that protection. It follows from this that we ourselves need instruction in these   5
matters, and could not and cannot answer all the questions which might be put to us. I ask you to ascribe this not to lack of goodwill but to lack of knowledge and certainty about the further handling of these matters.

I have since I first spoke about our colonial objectives stressed above all that a colonial policy is only possible when a majority of the nation believes in it with   10
conviction and determination. A regime which struggles laboriously to create colonies artificially against a powerful minority, or even a parliamentary majority, would be undertaking a labour of the Danaïdes [mythological figures condemned to fill a bottomless barrel] ...

H. Rothfels, *Bismarck und der Staat*, p. 77†

3.21   Bismarck's private motives in 1884

3.21(a)   A recent historian cites some of the contemporary evidence

It was in July 1884, significantly enough, that both the *Norddeutsche Allgemeine Zeitung* and Bismarck himself openly attacked the idea of a 'Gladstone ministry'

for Germany, under the aegis of the Crown Prince. Hence the constant emphasis
that the historian discovers being laid upon the domestic-political aspects of
Bismarck's colonial policy: sometimes put cynically, as when the Chancellor was   5
heard to tell one of his colleagues that 'All this colonial business is a sham, but
we need it for elections'; and sometimes more anxiously, as when, in the middle
of his campaign against the Radical-Clerical [Centre] majority in the Reichstag
which was voting down his various colonial projects but becoming nervous itself
about the 'national' agitation, the Chancellor informed Münster [German   10
ambassador in London] that 'for internal reasons, the colonial question ... is of
vital importance for us ... The smallest peak in New Guinea or West Africa,
though it may be quite worthless objectively, is at present more important for our
policy than the whole of Egypt and its future.' The more that the pro-
government press applauded the colonial annexations and responded with   15
approval to the anti-British manner in which it was being done, the greater
became the Bismarck family's conviction that they were on an electoral winner.
'Everything is now bubbling over on account of the colonial policy', wrote
Herbert Bismarck in August 1884 - so it would 'be wise to hold the elections
soon' before there was a swing to the Progressives. Here, as Holstein [an   20
important figure in the German foreign office] noted, both 'as a means of
combating foreign influences' and to check the 'liberals and democrats', was a
very substantial reason for supporting German interests overseas wherever they
appealed for help: 'the best card in the government's hand at present is definitely
a harsh move against England. One can hardly believe *how* popular it is in the   25
business world.'

P. M. Kennedy, *The Rise of Anglo-German Antagonism, 1860–1914*, p. 172

3.21(b)   Herbert Bismarck, foreign secretary, in conversation with Lothar von Schweinitz, German ambassador to Russia, in 1890

When we started colonial policy, we had to face a long reign by the Crown
Prince, during which English influence would predominate. In order to forestall
this, we had to launch a colonial policy, which is popular and can produce
conflicts with England at any moment.

A. J. P. Taylor, *The Struggle for Mastery in Europe*, p. 293

Questions

1   How far does **3.20** mark a change in the views Bismarck expressed about
    colonies in **3.18** and **3.19**?
2   In the light of **3.20**, **3.21(a)** and **3.21(b)** what considerations, in your
    view, best explain Bismarck's bid for colonies in 1884 and 1885?

4 The imperial regime at home, 1888–1914

On 9 March 1888 Kaiser Wilhelm I died, thus bringing to an end a partnership with Bismarck which had endured for twenty-six years. He was succeeded all too briefly by his son, Friedrich III, who was already suffering from cancer of the throat at his accession. Friedrich, married to Victoria, Queen Victoria's eldest daughter, was an anglophile and relatively liberal in his political views. It has been claimed that his early death was a tragedy not just for Germany but for Europe. Such a claim is impossible to test, but certainly the man who succeeded Friedrich after only three months, Wilhelm II, was very different from both his parents, both in character and outlook. He was to reign for thirty years until compelled to resign in 1918.

Wilhelm II was born in 1859. A difficult birth left him with a withered left arm which resisted all forms of medical treatment. His unremitting efforts to overcome this disability were remarkably successful. He became a good horsemen and a competent sailor. But his relations with his parents may have been affected and he was never the son they hoped for. His mother's preference for all things English grated on Wilhelm, who soon came to prefer the company of his grandfather and the Bismarck family. His education at the hands of an austere Calvinist tutor named Hinzpeter, at a grammar school in Prussian Hesse and at Bonn university made little impression beyond leaving Wilhelm with a taste for Greek culture. He was much more influenced by his experience of military life, first with the Prussian Foot Guards and then as colonel of the Guard Hussars. Unlike his father, who had fought in the Franco-Prussian war, Wilhelm's military service was confined to the parade ground and manoeuvres. It gave him an enthusiasm for uniforms and the externals of military life which he never lost.

More important were the ideas he imbibed, from whatever source, about the Prussian monarchy and its system of government. He saw himself as heir to Frederick the Great, both in his belief in a strong army (and in Wilhelm's case a strong navy as well) and in the virtues of absolute monarchy. 4.1–4.3 illustrate some of these characteristics.

4.1(a)   A letter from Princess Victoria of Prussia to Queen Victoria, August 1880

Willy is *chauvinistic* and *ultra* Prussian to a degree and with a violence which is very painful to me. I always turn off the subject or remain silent! With my own children I feel like a hen that has hatched ducklings.

4.1(b)   The same, 22 April 1887

He is *so* headstrong, so impatient of any control, except the Emperor's, and so *suspicious* of everyone who *might* be only a half-hearted admirer of Bismarck's that it is quite *useless* to attempt to enlighten him, discuss with him, or persuade him to listen to other people, or other opinions! Fritz [her husband] takes it profoundly *au tragique*, whilst I try to be patient and do not lose courage!

L. Cecil, *Wilhelm II, Prince and Emperor*, 1989, pp. 44, 81–2

4.2   An account of a visit to Munich by Wilhelm II in 1891

In mid-November Wilhelm infuriated his ministers and offended Bavarian susceptibilities when, during a state visit to Munich he signed the ceremonial Golden Book of the Rathaus, adding to his autograph the grandiloquent tag, '*Suprema lex, regis voluntas*' (the will of the king is the highest law). His mother was as shocked as any of his subjects: 'A Czar, an infallible Pope, the Bourbons   5 and our poor Charles I might have written such a sentence, but a constitutional Monarch in the 19th century ... .!!!', she wrote to Queen Victoria.

A. Palmer, *The Kaiser, Warlord of the Second Reich*, p. 54

4.3   A letter from Wilhelm II to Tsar Nicholas II, 25 October 1895

The French axiom that 'the King rules but does not govern' is basically false and revolutionary. I do not wish to rule in a merely nominal way and I will not do so, but instead intend to be the actual sovereign of my people.

L. Cecil, *Wilhelm II*, p. 226

Questions

1   How much faith would you put in Princess Victoria's assessment of her son's weaknesses **[4.1]**?
2   What can you infer about Wilhelm's conception of his role as emperor and king of Prussia from **4.1–4.3**?

How far Wilhelm was able to play the role he envisaged for himself depended on a number of factors, most obviously on his relationship with his ministers and on the balance of parties within the Reichstag. Wilhelm's own personality was also significant. His incessant desire to travel entailed long absences from Berlin; he lacked the powers of concentration, except when his attention was caught, to make him an effective ruler. Thus his powers tended to be used negatively rather than positively. The relationship with his chancellors was critical. It became obvious very soon after his accession that Wilhelm was not prepared to adopt the subservient attitude shown by his grandfather to Bismarck. Matters came to a head in January 1890 when at a meeting of a Crown Council Wilhelm insisted on putting forward his own policy for meeting working class grievances [4.4]. Bismarck was violently opposed to such measures and wanted a more severe anti-Socialist law instead. To these differences over policy was added a conflict over authority. Bismarck tried to resurrect a Prussian order of 1852 forbidding any minister from communicating with the emperor except through the chancellor. This Wilhelm flatly refused to concede. He insisted that Bismarck should either deliver the document in question or his resignation. Bismarck chose to resign [4.5(a), (b)]. Wilhelm had won the most important battle of his reign. All his chancellors thereafter knew that they must have the support of the All Highest if they were to survive. There would be no chancellor-dictatorship in Wilhelm's reign, but there were varying degrees of subservience.

General Leo Caprivi, appointed to succeed Bismarck in March 1890, was a professional soldier and administrator of moderate views [4.6]. He was prepared to pursue his own policies with respect to trade and defence, in the second case against Wilhelm's wishes. He promoted, unsuccessfully, a bill to allow Church authorities, both Lutheran and Catholic, greater control over education. He resisted Wilhelm's demand for a renewal of the Anti-Socialist Law in 1894. His opposition on this question has much to do with his resignation later that year.

Caprivi's successor was Prince Chlodwig zu Hohenlohe-Schillingsfürst (Hohenlohe) who, at the age of seventy-five, was as old as Bismarck had been at his resignation. There can be little doubt that he was appointed as a stop-gap until Wilhelm could find a successor in whom he could place his full confidence. Hohenlohe survived until 1900. He had little opinion of his capacity [4.7] but evidently was unwilling to surrender the material rewards that went with the job. He acquiesced in most of Wilhelm's requests, notably the cabinet changes made in 1897, though on one occasion in 1895 he and his fellow ministers did threaten collective resignation when Wilhelm initially refused to dismiss his reactionary minister of the interior, Ernst Köller, who had been suspected of leaking cabinet proceedings to the press.

Wilhelm gained his revenge in 1897, dismissing the relatively liberal minister of defence, General Walter Bronsart von Schellendorff and securing the replacement of his foreign secretary, Hermann Marschall von Bieberstein, by Bernhard von Bülow, the Kaiser's favourite.

Bülow became chancellor himself in 1900, already groomed for the post by Wilhelm's friend and confidante, Philipp von Eulenburg. According to his own testimony, Bülow wished only to serve the emperor [4.8]. When the two finally parted company in 1909 it was primarily because he had lost the emperor's support.

The last of Wilhelm's chancellors before 1914 was Theobald von Bethmann Hollweg, a man of very different stamp. He was a highly competent official who had served as minister of the interior first for Prussia and then for the empire prior to his appointment as chancellor. Like Caprivi, he was prepared to take an independent line, both with Wilhelm and his subordinates, but only, it would seem, to the point where he could secure Wilhelm's acquiescence, if not his approval. Bethmann Hollweg's career was to show that the doubts he expressed on his appointment [4.9] were all too well founded.

If authority ultimately rested with Wilhelm, the manner of its exercise was arbitrary and unpredictable. His irregular working habits and frequent absences from Berlin meant that his intervention in matters of policy could never be anticipated. He had no consistent domestic policies, suggesting concessions to the working classes in 1890 and repression in 1905, arguing in favour of tariff reductions in 1892 and for protection in 1904. Thus while his influence on policy can never be discounted it is not easy to assess its impact. 4.4–4.10 illustrate the relationship between Wilhelm and his chancellors, and the problems it raised.

4.4 Wilhelm's social policies announced to the Crown Council on 24 January 1890

What Wilhelm favoured was an abolition of Sunday work save where absolutely necessary, no night employment for women and children, no work by women in the last three weeks of pregnancy and for an equal period after giving birth, a pause in the workday for women to accomplish their domestic chores, their elimination from dangerous jobs, and limitation of labour by children under fourteen. Finally the government would support worker-employer committees that would cooperate with government inspectors to discuss discipline in factories and mines and the establishment of savings banks, churches, schools, hospitals and orphanages for the benefit of the labouring class.

L. Cecil, *Wilhelm II*, p. 152

4.5(a)   An excerpt from Bismarck's letter of resignation, 18 March 1890

[Bismarck refers to the order of 1852.] Since then, this order has been decisive in regulating the relationship of the Minister-President and the State Ministry, and it alone gave the Minister-President the authority which enabled him to take over responsibility for the policies of the cabinet, a responsibility demanded by the Landtag as well as public opinion. If each individual minister must receive   5
instructions from the monarch, without previous understandings with his colleagues, it becomes impossible in the cabinet to sustain uniform policies, for which each member can be responsible ...

On the aforementioned grounds, I am not in a position to carry out Your Majesty's demand, which would require me to initiate and countersign the   10
suspension of the order of 1852 recently brought up by me, and, despite that, at the same time carry out the presidency of the Ministry of State ...

Considering my attachment to service for the monarchy and Your Majesty and the long-established relationship which I believed would exist forever, it is very painful for me to terminate my accustomed relationship to the All Highest and to   15
the political life of the Reich and Prussia;

L. L. Snyder, *Documents of German History*, p. 267

4.5(b) *Punch* **comments on Bismarck's fall from power**

DROPPING THE PILOT.

Punch, **29 March 1890**

4.6 Caprivi's views on government in a letter to a friend some time after his resignation, 17 March 1895

From the beginning, I tried to encourage the Ministry of State to act like a corporate body, first so as to create a better substitute for the *personal* authority of Bismarck, second so as to be in a better position to offer resistance to the Kaiser's tendency to make sudden decisions.

J. C. G. Röhl, *Germany Without Bismarck*, p. 65

4.7 Hohenlohe bewails the difficulties of his position, 22 May 1897

Without authority, government is impossible. If I cannot get the Kaiser's consent to measures I regard as necessary, then I have no authority ... I cannot stay if H. M. removes Marschall against my will and if Holstein [head of the Political Department in the Foreign Office] goes. Likewise I cannot stay if the Kaiser appoints Ministers without consulting me ... I cannot govern against public opinion as well as against the Kaiser. To govern against the Kaiser and the public is to hang in mid-air. That is impossible.

J. C. G. Röhl, *Germany Without Bismarck*, p. 229

4.8 Bülow, in a letter to Philipp von Eulenburg, 23 July 1896

I would be a chancellor different than my predecessors. Bismarck was a power in himself ... Caprivi and Hohenlohe considered themselves as representatives of the 'government' and to a certain degree parliament. I [however] would regard myself as the accomplishing agent of His Majesty, in a way like his chief of staff. With me the personal regime would begin, in a good sense but also in actuality.

K. A. Lerman, *The Chancellor as Courtier*, p. 23

4.9 Bethmann Hollweg writes to a friend after his appointment as chancellor in 1909

You will find it natural that I accept this office with a heavy heart. Only a genius or a man driven by ambition and lust for power can covet this post. And I am neither. An ordinary man can only assume it when compelled by his sense of duty.

L. Cecil, *Wilhelm II*, p. 337

4.10 A recent biographer's view on Wilhelm II's rule

A *persönliches Regiment* [personal rule] under Wilhelm II existed only in the sense that, both before 1897 and for two decades thereafter, the parameters of movement that any chancellor or official possessed were determined by the Kaiser's likes and dislikes. Wilhelm did not, except rhetorically, issue orders but rather was pleased to allow or forbid, to appoint or to dismiss, according to his   5 ever-erratic moods. He was never the German autocrat, but rather the one constant, unavoidable, unpredictable factor with which all statesmen in Berlin, for better or worse, had to reckon. Governing therefore became a task of operating within those confines and using ingenuity to alter Wilhelm's opinions. Every chancellor or courtier found his way through this maze, for a time at least, and   10 there were episodes of good will and sometimes heady exultation, but eventually all of them, even the wily Bülow, annoyed the Kaiser and were coolly cast aside.

L. Cecil, *Wilhelm II*, p. 261

Questions

1 How far was Bismarck's resignation in 1890 prompted by differences over policy, how much by concern for his own power [**4.4**, **4.5(a)**]?
2 How aptly does **4.5(b)** summarise the political situation in Germany in March 1890?
3 What problems, according to **4.6** and **4.7**, were faced by Bismarck's successors in dealing with Wilhelm II?
4 In the light of **4.8** and **4.10** how significant a landmark was Bülow's appointment as chancellor in 1900?
5 How far do **4.6–4.9** support the description of Wilhelm II as 'the one constant, unavoidable, unpredictable factor with which all statesmen in Berlin ... had to reckon' [**4.10, lines 6–8**]?

Domestic policy choices

If between them Wilhelm II and his chancellors were the main initiators of policy, a third factor has to be added into the equation. The assent of the Reichstag, as we have seen, was needed for every substantive change in legislation and every new tax proposal. Mounting defence expenditure placed a growing burden on the imperial finances and the changing political complexion of the Reichstag made the task of coalition-building increasingly difficult. None of the chancellors who followed Bismarck succeeded in creating a solid bloc of supporters. Bülow came closest to doing so in the alliance he struck up with Conservatives, National Liberals and Progressives after the 1907 election, but the inherent contradictions within the bloc became all too apparent in the response to his tax proposals in 1908. The rise in support for the SPD and the continuing strength of the Centre Party [4.11] made the task of imposing policies which could command both the support of the Reichstag and the approval of Wilhelm II almost impossible.

In these circumstances, policy choices tended to depend on short-term considerations such as ability to cobble together a majority for a particular measure or the influence of powerful pressure groups such as the Navy League and individuals such as Tirpitz who were able to win all-party support for their initiatives. The remainder of this chapter is devoted to the choices that were made in three different areas: trade and finance, armaments and domestic reforms.

Trade and finance were closely linked. Tariffs provided the largest share of the empire's finances [4.13]. But pressure to raise tariffs for protective purposes came also from powerful pressure groups in the agricultural and industrial sectors. While Caprivi was successful in carrying through the Reichstag a reduction of duties on imported wheat and rye in exchange for favourable rates on exported German manufactures in 1891, there was mounting pressure to restore protection from agricultural interests, and in return for their support of Tirpitz's first Navy Law in 1898 they could rely on the backing of German iron producers. In 1902 Bülow bowed to these pressures, though not apparently himself convinced of the need for any such tariff increases [4.14]. The increase in the duties on imported wheat effectively barred Russian producers from the German market.

Germany's imperial revenue failed to meet expenditure from 1900 onwards, largely because of rising defence costs. Every suggested new tax was certain to meet opposition from one quarter or another. Indirect taxes were unpopular with the Liberals and the Social Democrats; taxes on property were anathema to the Conservatives; any form of direct taxation was likely to be opposed in the Bundesrat where the individual states resented any encroachment on their fiscal powers. Paradoxically the largest tax increase in the history of the empire before the First World War went through most easily in 1913, only because of a heightened sense of Germany's vulnerability during the Balkan wars (see pp. 103–5). By 1908 the national debt was almost twice what it had been in 1900 and Bülow made a determined effort to raise taxes, coupling an increase in taxes on consumer goods with an increase in the inheritance tax. Both the Conservative and Centre Parties opposed the latter proposal and it was defeated by eight votes on 24 June 1909. Bülow, who had already lost the Kaiser's confidence over the *Daily Telegraph* affair (see p. 90) tendered his resignation and it was left to his successor, Bethmann Hollweg, to reach a compromise, which involved the dropping of any increase to the inheritance tax.

From 1909 to 1912 defence spending was successfully contained, but an increase in the size of the army in 1912 led to further tax increases. Once again proposals were made to raise the inheritance tax, only to be abandoned in face of conservative opposition. However, in 1913 there was a much larger increase in defence spending, adding a further 136,000 men to the army's peacetime strength. This time Bethmann Hollweg introduced a tax on increases in the value of property, and by this device he was able to secure the support of the Left-Liberals and Social Democrats, despite the continuing opposition of the Conservatives [4.15].

The following documents show the changes in party strengths in the Reichstag [4.11, 4.12], imperial finances [4.13], Bülow's attitude to the tariff of 1902 [4.14] and Bethmann Hollweg's comments on his 1913 tax changes [4.15].

4.11   The composition of the Reichstag, 1890–1912

Party	1890	1893	1898	1903	1907	1912
Conservatives	73	72	56	54	60	43
Free Conservatives	20	28	23	21	24	14
National Liberals	42	53	46	51	54	45
Centre	106	96	102	100	105	91
Left-Liberals	76	48	49	36	49	42
Social Democrats	35	44	56	81	43	110
Poles	16	19	14	16	20	18
Danes	1	1	1	1	1	1
Alsace-Lorrainers	10	8	10	9	7	9
Guelphs	11	7	9	6	1	5
Anti-Semites	5	16	13	11	16	13
Others	2	5	18	11	17	6
Total	397	397	397	397	397	397
% voting			67.7	75.8	84.3	84.5

I. Porter and I. D. Armour, *Imperial Germany 1890–1918*, p. 111

4.12 *Punch* comments on the growing threat from socialism, 1907

FROM BISMARCK TO BUELOW.

A BIGGER TASK FOR A SMALLER MAN.

4.13   Germany's Ordinary Reich Revenue, 1901–1913 (million marks)

Source	1901	1906	1909	1913
Death duties		4.2	38.5	46.4
Capital gains				15.3
Stamp duties	84.0	138.6	171.4	258.6
Tariffs (a)	478.9	557.7	660.2	679.3
Taxes on consumption	333.2	378.4	485.7	659.7
Matricular contribution	15.2	24.2	48.5	51.9
Post office/railways	42.2	85.4	24.1	5.5
Reich Bank	12.8	29.2	16.4	34.7
Other (b)	94.4	93.3	196.6	229.9
Loans	332.8	258.4	639.0	109.3

(a) incl. tobacco, beer, sugar, spirits
(b) incl. Reich Stationery Office, administrative fees, fund income

V. R. Berghahn, *Modern Germany*, p. 295 (adapted)

4.14   Bernhard von Bülow writes to his press chief on the prospects of his Tariff Reform Bill, October 1902

Do you really believe that it is in my interest to bring about a speedy decision on the tariff question as the liberals wish? Is it not more advisable for me if the Tariff Bill comes to grief because of the left's obstruction or runs aground in some other way rather than is rejected by the Reichstag? ... The eventual success of the tariff is naturally preferable to all other outcomes if only because, with the   5
mood HM is in after the foolish attitude of the liberal newspapers during recent months, any crisis this winter could have incalculable consequences.

K. A. Lerman, *The Chancellor as Courtier*, p. 77

4.15   Bethmann Hollweg justifies his inheritance tax proposals in June 1913

In the Reichstag things are finally coming to a conclusion. I have been working for many months and in the end one loses one's energy and accepts stupidities just in order to finish things off. Our Imperial deputies have voted disgusting taxes ... Nevertheless stubbornness on my part would have been wrong. It is still a positive fact that this democratic Reichstag accepted such a gigantic military   5
bill.

K. H. Jarausch, *The Enigmatic Chancellor*, p. 98

Questions

1 Identify any clearly discernible trends in **4.11**.
2 Explain the message of **4.12**. What light does it shed on the perception of socialism in England and in Germany?
3 Compare total revenue in 1901 and in 1913 [**4.13**]. Which categories showed the largest increases and why?
4 What do the comments of Bülow and Bethmann Hollweg [**4.14, 4.15**] indicate about the problems they faced in handling the Reichstag and Wilhelm II?

Armaments policy

Despite the difficulties of increasing taxation Germany was still able to afford massive increases in her defences [**4.16**]. Spending on the army rose relentlessly, as it did in every European country except Britain, between 1890 and 1914. In 1874 appropriations for the army were voted for seven years at a time and even when this was reduced to five years in 1893, there was little the Reichstag could do to control them.

After the signing of the Franco-Russian alliance in 1894 and the virtual certainty that if war came Germany would be faced with two major opponents there was in any case little disposition to challenge the army's judgement of its needs. Those needs were based on the Schlieffen plan, the first version of which was produced as early as 1892 by Count Alfred von Schlieffen, chief of the German General Staff from 1891 to 1906. It was based on the premiss that in a two-front war with France and Russia, France must be defeated before the Russians had time to mobilise, and that the only way this could be achieved was by encirclement of the French army from the flank and the rear. This would necessarily entail a huge striking force which would advance through Luxemburg and Belgium, while another army would be needed to repulse the anticipated French advance through Alsace-Lorraine. While, naturally enough, details of the plan were not made available to the Reichstag, its members appreciated the danger of a combined Franco-Russian assault and, as we have seen, the major increase in defence spending in 1913 went through with little difficulty.

Another significant new departure in Germany's defence policy was the decision reached in 1898 to build a large battle fleet. Demands for a strong navy came from a variety of sources: merchants engaged in overseas trade, colonialists, powerful voices in the iron and shipbuilding industries. Wilhelm II had always been a keen sailor and was a fervent admirer of the British

Royal Navy, whose uniform he was proud to wear. It was the appointment of Admiral Alfred von Tirpitz as Secretary of the Navy in 1897, however, which provided the catalyst. Tirpitz was a convinced believer in the importance of sea power. He was one of the many disciples of Captain A. T. Mahan, 2,000 copies of whose book, *The Importance of Seapower in History*, were distributed in the campaign for the first Navy Law in 1897. In addition his political views helped to determine the shape the German navy was to take. Tirpitz, like his imperial master, had an ambivalent attitude to England. Admiration was mixed with jealousy. He sent his two daughters to Cheltenham Ladies' College between 1902 and 1904 but regarded the British navy as the biggest threat to Germany's independence. When he was appointed there were two schools of thought. One, supported initially by Wilhelm II, believed in the need for a large cruiser fleet which could defend Germany's colonies and trade routes. The other, of which Tirpitz was the chief exponent, believed that what Germany required was a large battle fleet capable of challenging any great power at sea, and thus strengthening Germany's bargaining position in international affairs [4.17]. Whether such a fleet was to be aimed primarily at Britain was not made clear in either of the Naval Acts, but other evidence suggests that it was [4.18]. What is beyond dispute is that as a consequence of the Navy Acts of 1898 and 1900 Germany was committed to the construction of a battle fleet of thirty-eight battleships, eight battle cruisers and twenty-four cruisers.

Why was the Reichstag so ready to support this initiative? Tirpitz was a highly skilled propagandist. In the autumn of 1897 he orchestrated a huge campaign in the press, organised the publication of pamphlets, and spread the word through schools, universities and even the Lutheran Church. After the passage of the first Navy Act in March 1898, with the support of the Centre Party, a Navy League was founded. Its purpose, according to its secretary, Viktor Schweinburg, was 'the emancipation of large sections of the political community from the spell of political parties by rousing their enthusiasm for this one great national issue' (Röhl, *Germany without Bismarck*, p. 255). By 1900 the Leagues's journal, *Die Flotte*, had a circulation of 300,000 and by 1906 the movement had over 1 million members.

It has also been argued that support for the navy was given by the agrarian interests in return for a higher tariff on agricultural imports and that the building of a navy would provide a cause around which all the anti-Socialist parties could rally (*Sammlungspolitik* [4.19]). The following documents illustrate the growth of German defence spending, the reasoning behind the decision to create a battle fleet and some of the arguments as to why that decision won such ready support.

4.16   German defence spending, 1870–1914, (£ million)

	1870	1880	1890	1900	1910	1914
Army	9.6	18.2	24.2	33.6	40.8	88.4
Navy	1.2	2.4	4.6	7.4	20.6	22.4
Total	10.8	20.6	28.8	41.0	61.4	110.8

A. J. P. Taylor, *The Struggle for Mastery in Europe*, pp. xxvii–xxviii, (adapted)

4.17   In his *Memoirs*, published in 1922, Tirpitz gives a variety of reasons for building a strong German navy

4.17(a)

Without sea-power Germany's position in the world resembled a mollusc without a shell. The flag had to follow trade, as other older states had realised long before it began to dawn upon us. As *The Fortnightly Review* put it, both tersely and correctly, in 1893: 'Commerce either engenders a navy which is strong enough to protect it, or else it passes into the hands of foreign merchants, who already enjoy such protection.'   5

4.17(b)

The plan of a German battle fleet was evolved without any idea of a war with England. It would have been madness both politically and strategically to have entertained the possibility of a later attack upon England. Before 1896 – that is, under Caprivi – the popular idea was, as I said, to regard England as the naval component of the Triple Alliance against France and Russia. There was also no   5 reason at that time to draw up defensive measures against England.

4.17(c)

The fundamental idea of this draft [on which Tirpitz was asked to comment in 1897] centred round *a foreign service fleet*. Now there were only a few States left in the world at that time such as Hayti, etc., in which any infringement of our rights could be corrected by foreign-service cruisers without giving rise to serious conflict. States like the Argentine already had modern warships at their disposal,   5 so that every foreign-service cruiser would have to be supported by a naval force in home waters, if it was to fulfil its purpose as an outpost. Moreover we had not one single foreign base. Throughout my whole career I have always had to oppose two ideas, especially beloved of the lay mind – the idea of a coastal

defence, and that of a cruiser fleet for foreign service. The world-war has proved   10
that the best *coastal defence* is a *battle fleet*. As to the cruiser war, I replied to the
Emperor at the time somewhat on the following lines: As a thorough-going
cruiser war and a war on the high seas against England and other great States is
altogether excluded by our lack of foreign bases and by Germany's geographical
situation – the foreign Admiralties know this quite well – what we need is a battle   15
fleet which can be stationed between Heligoland and the Thames.

4.17(d)

When working out the second Navy Bill, we hesitated for a long time whether or
not to bring the idea of the English menace into the preamble. I should have
preferred to leave England out of it altogether. But such an unusual demand as
was presented here, namely the doubling of our small naval force, made it
scarcely possible to avoid hinting at least at the real reason for it ... I decided,   5
therefore, in the preamble to the Navy Bill to give clear expression to the war
aim of the fleet, i.e. that of an honest political defensive, and I pointed out in the
Reichstag, in November 1899, that the most difficult war situation possible must
be taken as the basis for the size and composition of the German navy. This
would occur if we were opposed to the greatest of our possible opponents at sea.   10
To this end the fleet must be so constituted that its highest achievement, in a
war of defence, would lie in a naval battle in the North Sea ... Politically
speaking, however, the proposed German fleet offered the English every
guarantee of peace, because the latter were two or three times stronger, and it
would have been madness to have let loose a war with such slight prospects of   15
overcoming the British fleet.
   On the other hand, what we aimed at was to be so strong that it would mean a
certain risk even for the English fleet with its enormous superiority, to pick a
quarrel with us ... Thus, this idea of a *risk* which we hinted at was made more
popular in the shape of the formula that our navy was not to be maintained on a   20
bigger, nor on a smaller, scale, than would be necessary to make an attack upon
us seem a hazardous undertaking even to the greatest seapower.

Alfred von Tirpitz, *My Memoirs,* **vol. I, pp. 58–9, 67, 92, 123–4**

4.18   Tirpitz expressed himself somewhat differently in the plan submitted to Wilhelm II in June 1897

For Germany the most dangerous enemy at the present time is England. It is also
the enemy against which we most urgently require a certain measure of naval
force as a political power factor ... our fleet must be so constructed that it can
unfold its greatest military potential between Heligoland and the Thames ... The
military situation against England demands battleships in as great a number as   5
possible.

P. M. Kennedy, *The Rise of the Anglo-German Antagonism, 1860–1914,* **p. 224**

4.19   An extract from the memorandum appended to the German Naval Bill 1900

For the Protection of Sea Trade and Colonies There Is Only One Means – a Strong Battle Fleet. To protect Germany's sea trade and colonies in the existing circumstances there is only one means – Germany must have a fleet so strong that even for the adversary with the greatest sea power a war against it would involve such dangers as to imperil his position in the world.

L. L. Snyder, *Documents of German History*, **p. 283**

4.20   Some comments on the reasons for the Reichstag's support for the Navy Laws

4.20(a)

In March 1900, the American naval attaché in Berlin, who was familiar with the hard political bargains struck at home, knew what constellation of forces was necessary to get 'the bill for increased naval estimates through. The agrarians use their support for the bill to wring concessions to protect their own interests and, where possible, to get a tariff on agricultural imports which will be framed in   5
future trade agreements'. For some years previously, government ministries had been preparing for a new increase in protectionism. This came into effect with the Bülow tariff of 1902. In fact, the Supplementary Navy Bill and the customs tariff formed a package put together by the majority of deputies in the Reichstag. The middle classes and heavy industry were given a naval construction   10
programme, the large-scale agrarian producers a more favourable tariff system.

H-U. Wehler, *The German Empire*, **p. 168**

4.20(b)

This 'social imperialist' interpretation of government policy has been criticised first and foremost by Geoff Eley, who has pointed out how generalisations concerning the government's strategy have been applied to the period 1897–1909 without a firm basis of detailed research. Eley has argued that the relationship between agricultural protectionism and naval armaments (and, by implication,   5
Weltpolitik) was tactical and coincidental rather than strategic. Indeed, far from facilitating the emergence of a broad basis of government support, Tirpitz's naval plans highlighted the contradictions between industry and agriculture and helped to forge a coalition of forces hostile to the conservative *Sammlung* and committed to the expansion of the industrial economy.

K. A. Lerman, *The Chancellor as Courtier*, **p. 75**

Questions

1 How do you account for the differing rates of growth in spending on the army and the navy between 1900 and 1914 [**4.16**]?
2 How consistent are the arguments which Tirpitz advances for having a large battle fleet [**4.17**]?
3 In the light of **4.18** how justified was Tirpitz's claim in **4.17** that 'the proposed German fleet offered the English every guarantee of peace'?
4 With reference to **4.16–4.20** explain why the Reichstag was so ready to accept the first and second Navy Bills?

Domestic reform

When Bismarck resigned in 1890 it was still an open question whether Germany would evolve into a genuine democracy. By 1914 that question was no nearer resolution. Progress was made in some areas, while in others reforms were either not attempted or had to be aborted. Most worryingly, the period witnessed a disturbing growth in nationalist and racialist sentiment.

On the credit side the system of social insurance inaugurated by Bismarck was extended and expanded. In 1891 Sunday work was abolished and a guaranteed minimum wage introduced. In 1901 industrial arbitration courts were made compulsory in all towns with populations of over 20,000. Health insurance was extended to many more people in 1903 and further controls were imposed on child labour the same year. In 1911 insurance was extended to all salaried employees. By 1913 Germany could legitimately boast that it had a more comprehensive system of social insurance than either France or Britain [**4.21**].

On the political front a Polling Booth Law improved the secret ballot for Reichstag elections in 1904, and, equally significantly, from 1906 salaries were paid to the Reichstag deputies. British MPs were not paid until 1911. Alsace-Lorraine was given three seats in the Bundesrat in 1911 and universal suffrage was introduced there at the same time.

But against these gains have to be set the withdrawal of Caprivi's Schools Bill in 1892 and the failure to reform the Prussian electoral system. The Caprivi bill, whose main sponsor was Count Zedlitz, would have given both the Lutheran and the Catholic Churches greater control over the educational system. Wilhelm II was unwilling to rely on the Centre Party for the passage of the bill, and it was consequently withdrawn. The Prussian electoral system, which was both indirect and relied on an open ballot, as well as favouring the wealthy through the three class system was a constant obstacle to reform because the Prussian Diet continued to have a much more conservative composition than the Reichstag. Bülow made tentative moves towards reforming the system in 1908, in order to win liberal support, but the only serious attempt was Bethmann Hollweg's in 1909–10. This was limited enough. It would have ended indirect elections, and would have increased votes for educational and other qualifications, but the three class system and open voting were to be retained. Not surprisingly the measure was seen as too radical for the right and too timid for the left. Bethmann Hollweg's own attitude to the bill was ambivalent, to say the least [4.22], and it is not surprising that at the end of the day nothing was achieved.

It was, however, in its treatment of racial minorities that the German empire showed its most depressing face. The anti-Polish aspects of the *Kulturkampf* were continued by Bismarck's successors. Laws were passed to make German the only language of instruction in schools; through the Settlement Law of 1886 and the Expropriation Law of 1908 attempts were made to facilitate the purchase of Polish-owned land by German buyers. In July 1912 the Prussian government decided to implement the Expropriation Law, sequestering Polish estates. This led to an unparalleled vote of censure being passed in 1913 on Bethmann Hollweg in the Reichstag.

There was also a noticeable rise in anti-Semitic sentiment, fuelled by the publication of such works as Ernst Haeckel's *The Riddle of the Universe* and Houston Stewart Chamberlain's *Foundation of the Nineteenth Century*, both published in 1899. Wilhelm II was a warm admirer of Chamberlain. Anti-Semitic parties made their appearance and by 1907 had won sixteen seats in the Reichstag. One retired Bavarian general, Konstantin Freiherr von Gebsattel, was even prepared to advocate treating the Jews as aliens and removing their rights as citizens in a draft constitution which he sent to the Crown Prince in 1913 [4.23]. Bethmann Hollweg repudiated any such suggestion [4.24], but that it should have been made at all was surely a cause for concern.

A further example of the Imperial Government's insensitivity towards minorities is its handling of the Zabern affair. Trivial in itself, it has considerable symbolic importance. The Zabern affair was provoked by the insulting behaviour of a Prussian Lieutenant, Freiherr von Forster, towards an Alsatian recruit in Zabern whom he likened to a *Wacke* (screwball, blockhead). The incident occurred on 28 October 1913. It led to mounting friction between the garrison of Zabern and its civilian inhabitants, which culminated in the arrest of some thirty citizens by the military authorities for jeering at German officers on 28 November. In effect military power had superseded civilian rule. The Kaiser was determined to support the actions of the military as, with more reluctance, was Bethmann Hollweg [**4.25**]. In the debate held in the Reichstag on 4 December a vote of no confidence was passed on the chancellor by 293 votes to 54. It made little difference. The officers concerned were acquitted; Bethmann Hollweg retained his position. **4.21**–**4.25** reflect the mixed record of imperial governments in domestic reform.

4.21   German social insurance stands as a model without rivals

Fragen an die deutsche Geschichte, p. 237, Archiv der sozialen Demokratie (AdsD), Bonn, Bad Godesberg

4.22   Bethmann Hollweg and limited reform of the Prussian electoral system

4.22(a)   From a speech to the Lower House of the Prussian Landtag introducing the measure, January 1910

As long as the power of its royalty is unbroken Prussia will not let herself be dragged in the wake of parliamentarization ... Has not the democratization of parliament in all countries contributed to the brutalizing and dilution of political morals and to the hamstringing of progress which we need so dearly and to whose advancement suffrage reform is being introduced? ... not secret but public ballot contributes to a spirit of civic responsibility.

4.22(b)   His reflections after defeat of the bill, May 1910

'It is not easy in Germany to yield sufficiently but carefully enough to the pressure for democratic reform ... I could not and will not be able to make the law without the support of the Free Conservatives or National Liberals' ... [wanting to reform not discard tradition, the chancellor rejected the option of a Liberal-Center-Free Conservative majority because] ... 'it would in fact lead us too far to the left. Hence the problem remains unclear and dangerous, because with their personal, social, religious, and political hubris and intolerance, the Conservatives have succeeded in focusing everyone's disgust and dissatisfaction against the three class suffrage, which is generally seen as an expression of Junker predominance.'

K. H. Jarausch, *The Enigmatic Chancellor*, pp. 76–79

4.23   General Gebsattel's proposals for the treatment of Jews, October 1913

The Jews should be placed under the law pertaining to aliens and should remain the guests of the German people. Naturally they will be exempt from military service and will pay instead an army tax, which will perhaps be up to twice as high as the taxes paid by Germans. Obviously they will not be allowed to enter public service, to be judges, officials, university professors, lawyers, officers; they will however be allowed to become businessmen, directors of private banks, doctors.

J. C. G. Röhl, *From Bismarck to Hitler*, p. 50

4.24   Bethmann Hollweg's response to Gebsattel's proposals

The memorandum is also too superficial concerning the Jews. It simply declares them aliens and chases them out of the country, after having confiscated their property. It is not really possible to discuss such an idea seriously.

K. H. Jarausch, *The Enigmatic Chancellor*, p. 104

4.25 Bethmann Hollweg's defence of the military authorities in the Zabern affair

4.25(a)

The military authorities have always and justly believed that they cannot allow such insults as were directed against them, especially in this affair in which there was not a single incident but a whole chain of similar occurrences. Whether laws have been broken or whether monetary indemnity is forthcoming according to civil law, that must be left to the judiciary. Nevertheless, I beg you gentlemen   5
not to forget, in this serious and in many respects sad incident, that the Army has the right to protect itself against direct attack. It not only has the right, it has the duty. Otherwise, no army in the world could continue to exist.

L. L. Snyder, *Documents of German History*, p. 303

4.25(b) H-U. Wehler's conclusions on the Zabern affair

The powerlessness of the Reichstag to do anything, the military's open display of arrogance, the rapid collapse of the parliamentary opposition, and the defence of the army's traditional role in the state, all threw into sharp relief Germany's constitutional reality before 1914. They also highlighted the consequences of a social militarism which had seriously weakened any middle-class protest.

H-U. Wehler, *The German Empire*, p. 162

Questions

1 Compare the scale and range of provision made for the sick, the unemployed and the elderly in Germany in 1913 with that in France or Britain at the same time.
2 From the evidence of **4.22(a)** and **(b)** how serious was Bethmann Hollweg's commitment to reform of Prussian suffrage?
3 In the light of **4.24** what weight would you give to **4.23** as evidence for the strength of anti-Semitic sentiment in pre-war Germany?
4 What can be discerned about 'Germany's constitutional reality' from the Zabern affair [**4.25(a)**, **(b)**]?
5 How do you account for the progressiveness of German social legislation and the failure to reform German political institutions?

5 German foreign policy, 1890–1914

German foreign policy between 1890 and 1914 has been recently portrayed as dangerously aggressive and for that reason ultimately disastrous. Röhl wrote in 1967: 'The road which Germany took in 1897 led to diplomatic isolation, war, military defeat and the collapse of monarchy.' (*Germany without Bismarck*, p. 277). Fritz Fischer, in his analysis of German foreign policy from 1911 to 1914, first published in 1969, commented: 'There is no doubt that the war which German politicians started in July 1914 was not a preventive war fought out of "fear and despair". It was an attempt to defeat the enemy powers before they became too strong, and to realise Germany's political ambitions which may be summed up as German hegemony over Europe' (*War of Illusions: German Policy from 1911 to 1914*, p. 470).

This chapter seeks to investigate the justice of this indictment. If the German empire is to be held responsible for the outbreak of the First World War, that responsibility must rest not only with the politicians, but also with collective entities such as political parties and pressure groups and with the opinion formers such as writers and journalists who helped to influence the climate of opinion in which the decisions were taken. As we have already seen, post-Bismarckian Germany was in a state of constitutional and political flux in which power was widely dispersed. It might seem that after 1897 the emperor's authority was unchallenged, as Röhl has argued. But Wilhelm II's unpredictable behaviour and mercurial changes of attitude led to attempts to exclude him from policy making, notably after his indiscreet interview with the *Daily Telegraph* in 1907. He was positively encouraged to go on his usual North Sea voyage in July 1914 to keep him out of the way. While Bülow, a career diplomat before he became foreign secretary in 1897, could expect to play the leading role in foreign policy when he became chancellor in 1900, in practice he was much influenced by Friedrich Holstein, political advisor to the foreign office from 1876 until his resignation in 1906. Bethmann Hollweg, with no experience of foreign affairs, relied initially to a considerable extent on his foreign secretary, Kiderlen-Wächter, when he became chancellor. Others whose influence should never be discounted were the two chiefs of the Prussian General Staff during this period, Alfred Count von Schlieffen (1891–1906) and Helmuth von Moltke (1906–1914), and the navy secretary, Alfred von Tirpitz (1897–1916).

Harder to assess but certainly important was the influence of the right-wing pressure groups such as the *Alldeutscher Verband* (Pan-German League) and the writings of firebrands such as General Bernhardi [5.18] who helped to create a mood favourable to German aggrandisement. But while it may be possible to discern a common trend in German foreign policy during this period because those in power and the opinion-formers to whom they listened shared common objectives, responsibility for the particular decisions reached at any one time is much harder to locate. It may be that there was a deliberate bid for world power, *Griff nach der Weltmacht*, as Fischer argued in his book with that title, published in 1961. It may also be the case that German policy was characterised as much by contradictions and hesitations as by constant purpose during this period, and that dissenting voices were raised even if they were not heeded.

The first section of this chapter examines some of the evidence for the theory that Germany deliberately embarked on the pursuit of power, often characterised by the word, *Weltpolitik*. The initiatives taken under the umbrella of *Weltpolitik* and the course of German foreign policy in Europe between 1890 and 1912 are examined in the section '*Weltpolitik* in practice'. The chapter concludes by looking at German policy in the years of crisis, 1912–14, and the evidence of German responsibility for the outbreak of the First World War.

Weltpolitik

The literal translation of *Weltpolitik*, world policy, fails to do justice to the resonance of the term or to the associations with which it soon came to be invested. It has been defined as 'a coherent drive for world power' (Porter and Armour, *Imperial Germany*, p. 40), a definition which will serve for our purposes. The question then arises as to where and how this drive was to be made. Three obvious variants can be discerned: a straightforward bid for colonial possessions ('a place in the sun'); informal economic imperialism (the extension of German economic influence into areas such as the Balkans, the Far East and South America); and the exercise of German power in Europe either by the acquisition of land in the East (Lebensraum) or by the creation of a huge trading bloc (*Mitteleuropa*) under German leadership. These were not mutually exclusive objectives; politicians differed rather in the emphases placed on them. There were also differences over the methods by which they were to be achieved. Bethmann Hollweg, for instance, favoured the peaceful acquisition of colonies in Central Africa through negotiation; others, such as Kiderlen-Wächter, were prepared to use the threat of force, as in the Agadir crisis of 1911 [5.14, 5.15]. Others, such as Moltke and Admiral George von Müller, advocated a preventive war. The following documents illustrate some of these variants of *Weltpolitik* by those who believed in it. 5.1 is taken from the inaugural lecture given by Max Weber, the eminent sociologist, at Freiburg University in 1895. 5.2 is part of a memorandum given to the Kaiser's brother, Prince Henry, by Admiral Müller in 1896. Müller was to become chief of the naval cabinet in 1906, a post he held until 1918. 5.3 is an excerpt from the speech delivered to the Reichstag by Bülow in December 1897, following the German acquisition of the port of Kiaochow in China. 5.4, by way of contrast, indicates Bethmann Hollweg's own thoughts about the policies Germany should pursue.

5.1 Max Weber's inaugural lecture, Freiburg University, 1896

We must appreciate that the unification of Germany was a youthful prank indulged in by the nation in its old age and that because of its costliness it would have been better left undone if it was meant to be the end and not the starting point of a German policy of world power.

F. Fischer, *War of Illusions*, p. 32

5.2 Memorandum from Admiral Müller to Prince Henry, 1896

Here, too, our motto must be all or nothing. *Either* we harness the total strength of the nation, ruthlessly, even if it means accepting the risk of a major war, *or* we limit ourselves to continental power alone. The middle way of contenting ourselves with a few left-over pieces of East Africa and the South Sea Islands without any or at most an extremely limited suitability for settlement by   5
Germans; of maintaining a fleet too strong for the mere defence of our coastline yet too weak for the pursuance of *Weltpolitik* – all this implies a dispersal of our strength and a squandering of personal wealth which Caprivi's policy logically wished to see diverted to the army.

Will this policy turn out to have been right? We hope not. It would admittedly 10
bring the present nation comfortable days without serious conflicts or excitements, but as soon as our exports began noticeably to decline the artificial economic edifice would start to crumble and existence therein would become very unpleasant indeed.

J. C. G. Röhl, *Bismarck to Hitler*, p. 59

5.3   Bülow's speech to the Reichstag, December 1897

The times when the German left the land to one of his neighbours, the sea to the other, and reserved heaven, where pure doctrine is enthroned, for himself (*Laughter – Bravo!*) – those times are past. We regard it as one of our foremost duties, specifically in East Asia, to further and cultivate our shipping, our trade and our industry ...   5

We must demand that the German missionary and the German trader, German goods, the German flag and German ships in China are just as much respected as those of other powers. (*Lively Bravos!*) Finally we are perfectly prepared to take account of the interests of other great powers in the certain prospect that our own interests will meet with the same recognition they deserve.   10 (*Bravo!*) In short: we don't want to put anyone in the shade, but we demand our place in the sun too. (*Bravo!*) In East Asia as in the West Indies we will endeavour to safeguard our rights and our interests, true to the traditions of German policy, without unnecessary severity, but also without weakness. (*Lively applause.*)

I. Porter and I. D. Armour, *Imperial Germany*, pp. 94–5

5.4   Bethmann Hollweg's reflections on foreign policy, 1909

On all fronts we must drive forward quietly and patiently in order to regain that trust and confidence without which we cannot consolidate politically or economically. Of course this does not suit our irresponsible politicians, but according to my firm conviction, this is the only possible course for us. Then we shall be able to realize our greater aims in colonies and world trade without   5 having to risk our existence.

K. H. Jarausch, *The Enigmatic Chancellor*, pp. 110–111

Questions

1   What are the implications behind Max Weber's comments in **5.1**?
2   Why is Admiral Müller not prepared to see Germany limit itself to 'continental power alone' [**5.2**]?
3   Where is 'the place in the sun' referred to by Bülow in **5.3**?
4   How far do Weber, Müller, Bülow and Bethmann Hollweg share a common belief in *Weltpolitik*, and where do they differ?

Weltpolitik in practice

Behind the rhetoric, Germany's colonial gains between 1890 and 1914 were surprisingly meagre, at any rate by comparison with those made by Britain and France. Under Caprivi, Zanzibar was even abandoned in 1890 in exchange for the island of Heligoland in the North Sea. But there was a change of mood with Caprivi's departure. In 1897 Wilhelm II used the murder of two German missionaries in China as an excuse to send a German naval detachment to Kiaochow which was duly acquired as a treaty port. In 1899 an internal power struggle in Samoa, where Germany already had a foothold, led to the intervention of an Anglo-American mission and a dispute with Germany, resolved by the partition of the islands between Britain, Germany and the United States. In 1911 as a result of the second Moroccan crisis (see pp. 100–1) Germany acquired a substantial slice of the French Congo.

But if these were the total gains, they were by no means the end of German colonial aspirations. Many Germans cast covetous eyes at Central Africa and hopes were even entertained by Kiderlen-Wächter, foreign secretary from 1910 to 1912, of linking the Cameroons with German East Africa. This explains German interest in the Moroccan question and in the future of the Portuguese and Belgian colonies in Central Africa. Between 1911 and 1914 negotiations were conducted with the British government in the hope of establishing German claims to Angola and the Belgian Congo should the countries to whom these territories belonged prove incapable of ruling them [5.5]. When war broke out in 1914 German war aims soon came to include additions to her colonial possessions in Africa [6.11].

5.5   Richard von Kühlmann, councillor at the London Embassy and later foreign secretary, 1917–18, outlines the prospects for German colonial expansion to Bethmann Hollweg, 8 December 1912

It needs only a glance at a map to see that then [after the acquisition of large parts of the Portuguese colonies] only one indispensable corner-stone is required before the realisation of the great German colonial empire in Central Africa, and that is the acquisition of the Congo basin. It will hardly be necessary to demonstrate that this acquisition is desirable; it is the richest piece of Central Africa.   5

F. Fischer, *War of Illusions*, p. 311

Germany's imperial ambitions had inevitable consequences for her relations with the other European powers, usually for the worse. As in Bismarck's day, imperial policy was closely bound up with the European power balance and the need to win political support at home. Thus the pursuit of *Weltpolitik* had inevitable repercussions on the alliance system so carefully constructed by Bismarck. When Bismarck resigned in 1890 Germany was linked to Austria by the Dual Alliance and to Italy in the Triple Alliance. The 'line to St Petersburg' had been kept open by the Reinsurance Treaty. Only France was unreconciled. By 1894 France and Russia were firmly joined by a military convention and a formal alliance. In 1904 Britain and France resolved their colonial disputes in the Anglo-French entente, extended by the opening of military and naval conversations in 1905. In 1907 the third link in the chain was created with the Anglo-Russian entente. The Triple Alliance was now confronted by the Triple Entente.

How far was German policy to blame for this unfavourable outcome? This can best be investigated by examining German relations with each of her future antagonists. Of these, Russia was clearly seen as the most threatening, if only because of her comparative size. Wilhelm II has been blamed for the lapse of the Reinsurance Treaty in 1890, but it seems that in this instance it was rather his advisers who should take the responsibility [5.6]. Nor was this the end of attempts to maintain good relations with Russia. With the outbreak of the Russo-Japanese war in 1904 Wilhelm II saw the opportunity to win Russia's friendship again and, after a meeting at Björko with Nicholas II in July 1905, signed an agreement which might have paved the way to an alliance [5.7]. Bülow threatened to resign at what he took to be royal interference but the failure of the treaty may be ascribed as much to Russian reluctance as to German. Relations were not improved when Austria decided to annex Bosnia-Herzegovina in October 1908. Though Aehrenthal, the Austrian foreign minister, had tried to prepare the ground by holding conversations at Buchlau with the Russian foreign minister, Izvolski, Russia still felt betrayed. Significantly, Germany gave her unqualified support to Austria even though she had not been warned beforehand of Austrian intentions. Bülow assured Aehrenthal that: 'I shall regard whatever decision you come to as the appropriate one', and Moltke promised Conrad, the Austrian Chief of Staff, that 'the moment Russia mobilizes, Germany will also mobilize ...' (Taylor, *The Struggle for Mastery in Europe*, p. 453).

There was a further attempt at reconciliation in the meeting between Nicholas II and Wilhelm held at Potsdam in 1910, attended also by the new Russian foreign minister, the conciliatory Sergei Sazonoff. This yielded no specific agreement beyond tacit Russian acceptance of the Berlin-Baghdad railway. Its ulterior purpose may be gauged by Kiderlen-Wächter's comments [5.8].

5.6–5.8 indicate some of these shifts in German policy towards Russia.

5.6   Holstein's explanation for the lapse of the Reinsurance Treaty

And so a conference took place between the new Chancellor [Caprivi], Schweinitz [German ambassador to Russia] and Berchem, who had in the meantime taken over the direction of the Foreign Office after Herbert Bismarck's retirement. The relevant documents were produced and after examining them Schweinitz said they certainly contained things that were new to him. Under those circumstances   5 he thought it impossible to conclude this treaty with Russia because it would place us in a position inconsistent with other treaty obligations that were (at that time) still valid. I was not present at the conference but was told of its result immediately afterwards by Caprivi who had wasted no time in going to see the Kaiser. The Kaiser had said: 'If Schweinitz is also against it then it cannot be   10 done. I am extremely sorry, but I desire more than anything to pursue an honourable policy.'

Count Shuvalov had arrived in Berlin to renew the treaty in March 1890, but Bismarck resigned before this could be done. Holstein's own advice to Caprivi was not to renew the treaty.

N. Rich and M. H. Fisher, *The Holstein Papers,* **vol. 1, pp. 130–1**

5.7   The Björko Agreement, 24 July 1905

Their Majesties, the Emperor of all the Russias and the Emperor of Germany, as a means of maintaining the peace of Europe, have agreed upon the following articles of a treaty of defensive alliance:

ARTICLE I. In case one of the two Empires is attacked by a European power, its ally will come to its aid in Europe with all its sea and land forces ...

L. L. Snyder, *Documents of German History,* **p. 287**

5.8   An explanation for the failure of the Björko Treaty

In October 1904 and July 1905 Berlin proposed a Russo-German alliance which Paris would be encouraged or coerced into joining and which would have Britain as its target. In July 1905 the Treaty of Björko seemed to crown German efforts with success. Unfortunately for German hopes, however, Lambsdorff, Witte and the Grand Duke Nicholas Nikolayevich succeeded in persuading Nicholas II both   5 that the new treaty was incompatible with the French alliance and that Russian interests demanded that the latter be preserved.

D. C. B. Lieven, *Russia and the Origins of the First World War,* **p. 28**

5.9   Kiderlen explains German hopes at the Potsdam talks, 1910

Their [the Germans'] real concern was to disturb the Anglo-Russian entente. Kiderlen said Germany would not support an aggressive Austro-Hungarian policy in the Balkans, and asked a concession in return: 'The Russian Government declares that it is not committed [to] and that it does not intend to support a policy hostile to Germany which England might follow.' The Germans knew that   5 Russia would not support such a policy; what they wanted was written proof to show to the British, who could then be induced to make a similar declaration in their turn. Kiderlen wrote: 'The Russian assurance concerning relations with England is the alpha and omega for me of the whole agreement. It must be so drafted that it will compromise the Russians the day the English learn of it.'

Kiderlen was writing to Pourtalès, German ambassador to Russia, 4 December 1910. Kiderlen added: 'You had better burn this letter'.

A. J. P. Taylor, *The Struggle for Mastery in Europe,* **pp. 463–4**

Questions

1   How convincing is Holstein's explanation [5.6] for the lapse of the Reinsurance Treaty?
2   Why was the Björko agreement [5.7] so unpopular with both German and Russian governments?
3   What do 5.6–5.9 suggest about responsibility for the making of German foreign policy during this period?

Prior to 1890 Anglo-German relations had been reasonably harmonious, despite Bismarck's colonial ventures. In 1888 the Kaiser was even ready to extol the peace-keeping role of the British Royal Navy [5.10]. A deterioration set in with the Kruger telegram, despatched in January 1896. This arose out of the ill-fated Jameson Raid on the Transvaal in 1895, designed to provoke a rising which would thus enable Britain to annex the Boer Republic. Germany had quite strong links with the Transvaal, and even though the raid was a complete failure and Salisbury denied any prior knowledge of it, Wilhelm II felt the need to show his support for Kruger. Various possibilities were canvassed, including the wild suggestion that Germany should proclaim a German protectorate over the Transvaal. In the end the Kaiser was persuaded to send a telegram whose wording was more cautious than he had initially intended [**5.11**]. It was still sufficient to arouse a storm of protest in Britain and a flood of congratulatory messages to the Kaiser in Germany.

Though Germany observed a policy of neutrality in the Boer War, the Kruger telegram helped to give an anti-British orientation to the Navy Laws of 1898 and 1900. When Britain responded to the German naval challenge by building the first *Dreadnought* in 1906 a naval race was truly under way. It thwarted every subsequent effort to improve relations. Bethmann Hollweg was genuinely anxious to wean Britain away from the Triple Entente and made a serious effort to do so during the Haldane mission to Germany in the spring of 1912, even at one point threatening to resign if Tirpitz persisted with his plan to build a further three German battleships. But in return for scrapping this projected increase in the German navy Bethmann Hollweg insisted on a pledge of British neutrality in the event of war. This was further than Britain was prepared to go [**5.12(b)**]. **5.10–5.12** illustrate these changes in Anglo-German relations between 1888 and 1912.

5.10 A letter from Wilhelm II to Lord Charles Beresford, a British admiral, 20 December 1888

A strong and well armed and ably commanded British fleet is an absolute necessity for the welfare of Europe and the maintenance of peace.

L. Cecil, *Wilhelm II*, p. 276

5.11 The Kruger telegram, 3 January 1896

I express my sincere congratulations that, supported by your people, without appealing for the help of friendly powers, you have succeeded by your own energetic action against armed bands which invaded your country as disturbers of the peace, and have thus been enabled to restore peace and safeguard the independence of your country against attacks from the outside. WILHELM I. R.   5

In connection with the Kruger telegram, *The Times* correspondent, Valentine Chirol, commented according to Holstein, 'After our recent experience of the mood both of the Kaiser and the people in Germany the British government will be inclined to go much further than it hitherto intended in the way of concessions or even considerable sacrifices, in order to create better relations with   10 France.'

N. Rich and M. H. Fisher, *The Holstein Papers*, vol. 1, p. 170

5.12(a)   Bethmann Hollweg's draft for a German-British agreement, 12 March 1912

If either of the High Contracting parties become entangled in a war with one or more powers in which it cannot be said to be the aggressor the other of the High Contracting parties will at least observe towards the power so entangled a benevolent neutrality and use its utmost endeavours for the localisation of the conflict. The High Contracting parties undertake to inform each other on their   5 attitude should one of them be forced to declare war on a third party through open provocation.

5.12(b)   The British foreign secretary Sir Edward Grey's response to this formula, 17 March 1912

England declares that she will neither make nor join in any unprovoked attack upon Germany and pursue no aggressive policy towards her.

F. Fischer, *War of Illusions*, p. 130

Questions

1   How important was the Kruger telegram [5.11] in worsening Anglo-German relations?
2   What were the essential differences between Bethmann Hollweg's draft for an Anglo-German agreement and Grey's response [5.12(a), (b)]?
3   On whom should the main responsibility lie for the deterioration in Anglo-German relations between 1890 and 1914?

So long as Germany continued to occupy Alsace-Lorraine France remained a potential enemy. With the signing of the Franco-Russian alliance in 1894 what had been a worrying possibility now became a virtual certainty: in any war with France Germany would also have to contend with Russia. With the signing of the Anglo-French entente in 1904 there was now a distinct possibility that Britain would also come to France's support. In these circumstances it might have been expected that Germany would pursue a more conciliatory policy towards France. There is little indication that she tried to do so. German efforts seem rather to have been devoted to breaking up the entente.

Whereas Bismarck had been ready to encourage French colonisation in North Africa as a way of dividing Britain and France, in the two Moroccan crises of 1905 and 1911 German policy had the reverse effect. The first crisis arose out of the Anglo-French agreement of April 1904, recognising France's claim to a preponderant say in the government of Morocco. Holstein and Bülow decided to challenge this claim and persuaded the Kaiser to make a symbolic gesture by paying a ceremonial visit to the Sultan at Tangier in March 1905 [5.13]. After much posturing and the resignation of the French minister responsible for the Morocco agreement, Delcassé, an international conference was held at Algeciras in 1906 at which Germany found herself isolated and France's claims were recognised. Whether certain elements in Germany were anxious to provoke a war with France at this stage is far from clear [5.14].

A more serious crisis occurred in 1911. Disorders in the town of Fez prompted the French to send a relief expedition to the city. Germany interpreted this action as a breach of the Algeciras agreement, and therefore an excuse for Germany to seek compensation, if not in Morocco then in French West Africa. Kiderlen, who appears to have been the inspiration behind this policy, urged that Germany should seize the ports of Agadir and Mogador because 'in possession of such a pawn we can watch quietly and await further developments in Morocco, whether for example France will offer us suitable compensation from its colonial possessions in return for which we could then evacuate the two ports' (Fischer, *War of Illusions*, p. 72). The Kaiser and Bethmann Hollweg gave their approval and on 1 July the German gunboat, *Panther*, arrived at Agadir. There were strong protests from Britain as well as France, and on 21 July Lloyd George with the approval of the British cabinet delivered a powerful warning to Germany in a speech at the Mansion House. In the event, an agreement was signed on 4 November under which Germany was 'compensated' for France's enhanced role in Morocco with a considerable slice of the French Congo, much of it desert or swamp. Much of the debate in the Reichstag which followed this agreement reflected the popular demand for German expansion and disillusion with the paltriness of the gains achieved [5.16]. The following documents provide a commentary on German policy during the two Moroccan crises.

5.13 An account by Baron von Schoen, a member of the imperial entourage, of Wilhelm II's visit to Tangier, 31 March 1905

After surmounting not insignificant technical landing difficulties at Tangier, we were given a very dignified reception at the dock by Moroccan authorities and German colonists ...

Conversations with the French *Chargé d'affaires* at first likewise indifferent. When this person, however, presented the respect and greetings of Delcassé and,   5 so to speak, welcomed His Majesty to Morocco, the response:

The visit of the All Highest means that His Majesty demands free trade for Germany and complete equality of rights with other nations; when Count Cherisey [the French *Chargé d'affaires*] wanted magnanimously to concede this, His Majesty remarked that he would come to an understanding with the Sultan   1(as a free and independent ruler of an independent country, that His Majesty himself would know how to bring his influence to make valid his rightful claims, and expected that this would be respected also by France. Count Cherisey went pale, wanted to reply, but, prevented by a curt dismissal, he left with his head lowered.

L. L. Snyder, *Documents of German History*, **p. 289**

5.14   Holstein reflects on the reasons for the Kaiser's visit to Tangier in a conversation with a fellow diplomat, von der Lancken, in 1909

But when I began fully to appreciate this danger [that Britain might be drawn into the Franco-Russian alliance] I became convinced that before we were strangled by the circle of other great powers we must use all our energy to break this circle and in so doing must not shrink back even from the ultimate step. Hence the Emperor's visit to Tangier. But I was wrong in my estimate of the   5 personality of the man who takes the final decision. I should have realized that Prince Bülow would be reluctant and His Majesty unwilling to take the final step.

F. Fischer, *War of Illusions*, **p. 56**

5.15   Karl Riezler, Bethmann Hollweg's private secretary, comments in his diary on Kiderlen's role in the Agadir crisis

'Kiderlen informs nobody, not even the chancellor', Riezler complained about the foreign secretary's secretiveness. 'He speaks when he likes, but not when he should. Bethmann said yesterday, he wanted to give Kiderlen a lot to drink in the evening to find out what he ultimately wants.' The stratagem worked, but 'what he said was very serious, so that the chancellor believes Kiderlen not only   5 considers the possibility of war but wants it ... Kiderlen's stubbornness is the most important political factor at present. It is elemental and unruly. Considering the confidence that he enjoys, neither the chancellor nor the Kaiser can let him go.'

K. H. Jarausch, *The Enigmatic Chancellor*, **pp. 122–3**

5.16   The debate on the Morocco Agreement in the Reichstag, 9–10 November 1911

5.16(a)   Ernst Bassermann, a leading figure in the National Liberal Party

This agreement fails to take account of Germany's interests, of the position and resources of the German empire ... we grant France the Protectorate; it is a wicked result.

5.16(b)   Bethmann Hollweg

Forces have been at work everywhere which have more to do with the impending elections than with Morocco or the Congo ... But to inflame national passions to boiling point for the sake of utopian schemes of conquest or party purposes is to compromise patriotism and to waste a valuable asset.

F. Fischer, *War of Illusions,* **p. 91**

Questions

1   Comment on the reasons for the Kaiser's visit to Tangier implied in **5.13** and **5.14**.
2   Which of these sources would you regard as the more reliable and why?
3   How far do **5.15** and **5.16** suggest that public opinion supported German actions in the Agadir crisis?
4   To what extent do **5.13–5.16** support the view that German policy in North Africa between 1905 and 1911 was governed as much by fear of encirclement as by territorial ambition?

The approach of war, 1912–14

Whereas the two Moroccan crises of 1905–6 and 1911 and the Bosnian annexation crisis of 1908–9 had all been resolved peacefully, the assassination of Franz Ferdinand on 28 July 1914 led within five weeks to the outbreak of the First World War. Various explanations have been offered for this outcome. Lloyd George argued in the first volume of his *War Memoirs,* published in 1933, that 'the nations in 1914 slithered over the brink into the boiling cauldron of war without any trace of apprehension or dismay' and that 'Amongst the rulers and statesmen who alone could give the final word which caused great armies to spring from the ground and march to and fro across frontiers, one can see now clearly that not one of them wanted war' (D. Lloyd George, *War Memoirs*, vol. 1, pp. 52–5). This view seems now largely discredited: 'Historians are in 1969 in general agreement that in the summer of 1914 the German empire risked a preventive war' (Fischer, *War of Illusions*, p. 461). But Fischer goes further. He states later on in the same book that after the assassination attempt 'the German government was determined from early July 1914 onwards to use this favourable opportunity for a war against France and Russia' (p. 480). Even if Fischer's arguments are correct, it still has to be explained why Germany, which was not prepared 'to take the ultimate step' in 1905 or 1911, was ready and anxious to do so in 1914.

Among the reasons given have been the worsening position of right-wing forces in Germany, which sought salvation in a popular war, and the increasing instability of the international situation, especially in the Balkan peninsula where the collapse of Turkish rule removed 'a shock absorber in the international system' (R. Henig, *The Origins of the First World War*, p. 41). Before examining the evidence for these propositions, a brief summary of the crowded events of these years is necessary. On the domestic front January 1912 witnessed a general election in which the Social Democrats gained a third of the vote and 110 seats in the Reichstag. Together with the 91 seats won by the Centre party, Bismarck's *Reichsfeinde* now controlled over half the seats. The tone of the nationalist and racialist press grew increasingly strident; the calls for a preventive war more frequent and from more respected sources [5.18, 5.19]. On the other hand, in December 1913 Bethmann Hollweg, as we have seen, was the victim of a vote of no confidence (293 to 54) in the Reichstag because of his handling of the Zabern affair. It seemed that positions in Germany were becoming increasingly polarised and that a successful war might be the only way to restore a sense of unity.

The growing sense of tension within Germany reflected an international scene that was equally disturbed. In the summer of 1912 the Balkan League, made up of Bulgaria, Serbia, Greece and Montenegro, was formed under the benevolent patronage of Russia. In October the League declared war on Turkey, a war which ended only after the intervention of the powers with the treaty of London in May 1913. Two months later the victors fell out over the spoils and a further war broke out, this time between Bulgaria on one side and Serbia, Greece, Montenegro and a revived Turkey on the other. This war ended officially in October 1913 with the treaty of Bucharest, but arguments continued over the implementation of its terms. The territorial changes arising from these wars are summarised in **5.17**. Most significant from our point of view are the gains made by Serbia, still barred however from access to the Adriatic through the creation of Albania, at Austria's insistence.

A further crisis was provoked in November 1913 by the despatch of a German military mission to Turkey headed by General Liman von Sanders, who was also put in command of a Turkish army corps at Constantinople. This, needless to say, raised Russian fears over German control of the Straits, and tension was only removed when von Sanders was 'promoted' to the post of Inspector General of the Turkish Army, which took him away from Constantinople. The increasing international tensions of these years was reflected in the alarmist tone of much right-wing opinion, represented here. **5.18** is taken from a book by General Friedrich von Bernhardi, *Germany and the Next War*, published in 1912. It went through nine editions by 1914. Bernhardi was at the time commander of VII Army Corps. **5.19** is taken from an article published in *Post*, on 24 February 1914. *Post* was the party organ of the Free Conservatives.

5.17   The Balkans 1912–13

N

BOSNIA
(Annexed to
Austria 1908)

Sarajevo ●

Belgrade ●

S E R B I A

Nish ●

Bucharest ●

R U M A N I A

Pruth

Silistria ●

D O B R U J A

Danube

Varna ●

B U L G A R I A

Sofia ●

MONTENEGRO

Cetinje ●

Scutari ●

Kumanovo ●

Chatalja
Lines

Adrianople ●

Kirk
Kilisse ●

Midia ●

ALBANIA
(Indep. 1913)

Durazzo ●

Monastir ●

M A C E D O N I A

Kavalla ●

T H R A C E

Lule Burgas ●

Constantinople ●

Florina ●

Dedeagach ● Enos ●

Salonica ●

Janina ●

EPIRUS

G R E E C E

IMBROS

LEMNOS

MITYLENE

Athens ●

CHIOS

SAMOS

DODECANESE
(Ital. occup.)

Acquired from Turkey by:

Serbia

Greece

Bulgaria

Montenegro

To Rumania
from Bulgaria

CRETE

0   100   200   300 km

5.18   *Germany and the Next War* by General Friedrich von Bernhardi

If the Imperial Government was of the opinion that it was necessary in the
present circumstances to avoid war [the Agadir crisis], still the situation in the
world generally shows there can be only a short respite before we once more face
the question whether we will draw the sword for our position in the world or
renounce such position once and for all. We must not in any case wait until our   5
opponents have completed their arming and decide that the hour of attack has
come.

   We must use the respite we still enjoy for the most energetic warlike
preparations according to the principles I have already laid down. All national
parties must rally round the government, which has to represent our dearest   10
interests abroad ... We may expect from the Government that it will prosecute
the military and political preparations for war with the energy which the situation
demands in clear knowledge of the dangers threatening us, but also in correct
appreciation of our national needs and of the warlike strength of our people, and
that it will not let any conventional scruples distract it from this object.

General Friedrich von Bernhardi, *Germany and the Next War*, pp. 287–8

5.19   Austria and the Triple Alliance: an article in *Post*, 24 February 1914, quoted by Fischer

France is not yet ready to fight, England is involved in domestic and colonial
difficulties. Russia shuns war because it is afraid of revolution at home. Are we to
wait until our opponents are ready or shall we seize a propitious moment to bring
about a decision? That is the pregnant question which must be decided. [After
surveying the position of Germany's allies the article continues:] We therefore   5
hold the trump cards and with a determined offensive we could take charge of
European policy and safeguard our future.

   This is not to say that we should begin a future war; but if there is a conflict
of interests we must not give way but risk a war which we should start with a
determined offensive, be it over a new Morocco, over the position of General von   10
Liman or over near Eastern issues; the pretext is unimportant because what
matters is not this, but that our whole future is at stake.

   [Fischer comments] It should be pointed out that 'These articles in *Post* found
almost no echo in the German press', but an article in a more responsible
newspaper, the *Kölnische Zeitung*, published on 2 March 1914 concluded: 'We   15
know where we stand ... But let us hope that these manifestations of official
Russian policy destroy once and for all the legend of the historic German-Russian
friendship.'

F. Fischer, *War of Illusions*, pp. 372–4

Questions

1   How close do **5.18** and **5.19** come to advocating a German declaration of war?
2   What value would you give to **5.18** and **5.19** as a gauge of public opinion in Germany between 1912 and 1914?

German policy throughout these events was a mixture of conciliation and threat. Bethmann Hollweg played a constructive role in the negotiations which led to the ending of the Balkan wars. At the same time the voices calling for a preventive war grew more persistent. Nothing perhaps better illustrates the ambiguity of German policy at this time than the so-called War Council that was held on 8 December 1912. It was evidently convened because of a letter from Prince Lichnowsky, German ambassador in London, to Bethmann Hollweg in which he indicated that Britain would not be 'a 5 quiet bystander' in a war between Austria and Serbia; that 'the balance between the various groups must be more or less preserved', and that Britain 'could therefore in no circumstances allow France to be crushed'. Wilhelm II reacted furiously. He commented: 'What a nation of shopkeepers! This is what is called a peace policy! Balance of power! The final struggle between 10 the Slavs and the Teutons will see the Anglo-Saxons on the side of the Slavs and the Gauls (Fischer, *War of Illusions*, p. 160).

The Council was attended by Moltke, Tirpitz, Heeringen (chief of the Admiralty Staff) and Müller (chief of the Naval Staff). Various accounts of 15 this celebrated meeting have survived. Two versions are reproduced here, as are Bethmann Hollweg's comments [**5.20–5.21**].

5.20   Two accounts of the War Council held on 8 December 1912

5.20(a)   Admiral von Müller's diary

The Chief of the Great General Staff [Moltke] says: war the sooner the better, but he does not draw the logical conclusions from this which is to present Russia or France or both with an ultimatum which would unleash the war with right on our side ... The result was pretty well zero.

5.20(b)   On 12 December the Saxon military attaché, Leuckart, reported on the information given to him by the Prussian Ministry of War

His Excellency von Moltke wants war because he believes that at the moment it would not be convenient to France as is shown by advocacy of a peaceful solution. Admiral von Tirpitz, on the other hand, would prefer it to come in a year's time when the Canal [the Kiel canal] and the submarine harbour in Heligoland will be ready.

F. Fischer, *War of Illusions*, pp. 162–3

5.21   Bethmann Hollweg comments on the Conference

Although William II claimed that the chancellor 'had now gotten used to the idea of war', Bethmann denounced the impromptu meeting as an impetuous creation of fear. 'Haldane's communication to Lichnowsky was not nearly that serious. It only affirmed what we have long known: *now as before England follows a policy of balance of power and therefore will stand up for France if the latter is in danger of* 5 *being annihilated by us* ... Demanding that England throws herself around his neck, despite his policy H.M. has gotten terribly excited about this and immediately held a war council with his stalwarts of army and navy behind my and Kiderlen's back, ordered the preparation of an army *and navy* increase and broadcast the Haldane conversation, fantastically enlarged, over the whole world 10 ... Britain wants no continental war because it would be drawn into it and does not want to fight. In that light its obligations toward France have their positive side. But we must not conduct a nervous jumping-jack policy; otherwise the others' patience will run out one day.'

K. H. Jarausch, *The Enigmatic Chancellor*, pp. 134–5

Questions

1   How reliable a record do **5.20(a)** and **(b)** provide of the War Council's proceedings?
2   In view of the comments of Admiral Müller and Bethmann Hollweg, what importance would you give to the War Council in determining future German policy?

The July crisis

The final crisis which precipitated the outbreak of the First World War has been, and continues to be, the subject of intense investigation, speculation and controversy. It has generated thousands of documents, books and articles.

Any selection of sources is bound to be arbitrary and possibly tendentious. Those chosen here are no exception. All that has been attempted is to focus on three decisions relating to German responsibility for the war: first the decision to give unequivocal support to Austria in her treatment of Serbia after the assassination of Franz Ferdinand; secondly the negative response to offers of mediation once the ultimatum to Serbia had been delivered; and finally the decision to extend the war to Russia and then to France and Belgium. In each case the context of the decisions will be outlined before the relevant sources are presented.

On 28 June 1914 the Archduke Franz Ferdinand and his wife were assassinated while on a state visit to Sarajevo. The identity of the assassin was not in doubt. The culprit, Gabriel Princip, was apprehended immediately. The Austrian government suspected, but could not prove, the complicity of the Serbian government. Militants such as Conrad put pressure on the emperor to seize this opportunity to crush Serbia. On 2 July Franz Joseph drew up a letter which was despatched to Berlin with a special courier, Count Hoyos, requesting German support in the measures being contemplated. War was not mentioned but, in a critical phrase, it was argued that a regrouping of Balkan powers favourable to Austria could be achieved only 'if Serbia ... is eliminated as a political factor in the Balkans' (F. Fischer, *War of Illusions*, p. 476). The Kaiser met Hoyos on the morning of 5 July, and conferred with Bethmann Hollweg in the afternoon. How far Germany was already anticipating a war can perhaps be gauged by the note made by the Austrian Foreign Office of a conversation that had already taken place on 4 July between Tschirschky, the German ambassador in Vienna, and the section chief in the Austrian Foreign Office, Count Forgach [5.22]. The official German response, often described as a blank cheque, was sent by Bethmann Hollweg to Tschirschky, on 6 July [5.23]. Bethmann Hollweg seems to have gone rather further in the assurances he gave to the Austrian ambassador in Berlin, Szögyényi [5.24].

5.22   Note by Count Forgach, 4 July 1914

Even if the German press which today is totally anti-Serb were again to advocate peace Vienna must not allow itself to be confused. The Emperor and the Empire would certainly stand by Austria-Hungary. No Great Power could speak more frankly to another.

F. Fischer, *War of Illusions*, p. 476

5.23 Bethmann Hollweg's despatch to Tschirschky, 6 July 1914

Finally, as far as concerns Serbia, His Majesty, of course, cannot interfere in the dispute now going on between Austria-Hungary and that country, as it is not a matter within his competence. The Emperor Francis Joseph may, however, rest assured that His Majesty will, under all circumstance[1] faithfully stand by Austria-Hungary, as is required by the obligation of his alliance and ancient friendship.   5

[1] *'under all circumstance': this phrase in the original draft, the work of Zimmerman, acting foreign secretary, was omitted in the final version by Bethmann Hollweg.*

L. L. Snyder, *Documents of German History*, pp. 310–11

5.24 Szögyényi, the Austrian ambassador in Berlin, comments on his interview with Bethmann Hollweg on 6 July

Although he had always advised us to get along with Serbia, after the recent events he understood that this was well nigh impossible. In the course of further conversation I realized that the chancellor, like his imperial master, considers our immediate intervention against Serbia the most radical and the best solution to our difficulties in the Balkans.

K. H. Jarausch, *The Enigmatic Chancellor*, p. 156

Questions

1 In the light of **5.22–5.24** how appropriate is the term 'blank cheque' used to describe Germany's assurances to Austria on 6 July 1914?
2 How far do **5.22–5.24** suggest that Austria was being pressed to take a firm line with Serbia?

Vienna proceeded to act on the advice given in **5.24**. An important ministerial council was held on 7 July at which, with the exception of Count Tisza, prime minister of Hungary, there was unanimous support for taking a strong line with Serbia even at the risk of Russian intervention. On 14 July agreement was reached on the terms of the ultimatum to be delivered to Serbia, but its delivery was to be postponed until 25 July to enable the projected visit of the French president and prime minister to St Petersburg to be completed before the news broke. Meanwhile, at Berlin, preparations for German mobilisation were set in train. On 19 July the final terms of the ultimatum were agreed in Vienna. It was now to be delivered on 23 July at 5.00 p.m., and a time limit of forty-eight hours was specified. Germany was kept fully apprised of all these developments.

The ultimatum was framed so as to be unacceptable to the Serbs. Grey, the British foreign secretary, described it as 'the most formidable document that I have ever seen addressed by one state to another that is independent' (Z. Steiner, *Britain and the Origins of the First World War*, p. 222). He immediately embarked on a succession of initiatives, first to defuse the quarrel between Austria and Serbia, and then, when that looked impossible, to localise the impending conflict. Germany discouraged all these initiatives [**5.25**]. In Russia there was a similar sense of alarm. The prime minister, Sazonoff, convened a ministerial council on 24 July at which it was decided to support Serbia in any actions taken against her by Austria. The French president, Poincaré, was at sea returning from St Petersburg on 24 July and did not reach French soil until 29 July. France could thus do little to bring her influence to bear.

There can be little doubt that once the ultimatum had been delivered, Austria, at any rate, was bent on war. The Austrian ambassador to Belgrade left his post as soon as the conciliatory Serbian reply had been received on 25 July. The confusion in German policy can be illustrated by the Kaiser's response to the Serbian reply, which he saw on 28 July: 'A brilliant performance for a time limit of only forty eight hours. This is the most that one could have expected; but with it every reason for war disappears ... (Snyder, *Documents of German History*, p. 326). He at once urged Bethmann Hollweg to submit a proposal to be put to Austria [**5.26**]. But by the time it was received Austria had already declared war on Serbia and Belgrade had been bombarded. Whether or not Germany played a restraining role after the despatch of the ultimatum can perhaps be gauged by the following documents.

5.25   The Kaiser's marginal notes on Grey's proposal for mediation between Austria and Serbia by the four nations not immediately concerned: England, Germany, France and Italy, 25 July 1914

This is superfluous, as Austria has already made matters plain to Russia and Grey has nothing else to propose. I will not join in it unless Austria expressly asks me to, which is not likely. In *vital* questions and those of honour one does not consult with others.

I. Geiss, *July 1914: The Outbreak of the First World War: Selected Documents*, p. 184

5.26   Telegram from Bethmann Hollweg to Tschirschky, 28 July 1914

The reply of the Serbian government to the Austrian ultimatum, which has now
been received, makes it clear that Serbia has agreed to the Austrian demands to
so great an extent that, in case of a completely uncompromising attitude on the
part of the Austrian government, it will become necessary to reckon upon the
gradual defection from its cause of public opinion throughout all Europe ... if it   5
[the Imperial government] continues to maintain its previous aloofness in the face
of such proposals [of mediation], it will incur the odium of having been
responsible for a world war, even, finally, among the German people themselves.
A successful war cannot be commenced and carried on on any such basis. It is
imperative that the responsibility for the eventual extension of the war among   10
those nations not immediately concerned should, under all circumstances, fall on
Russia ...

You will have to avoid very carefully giving the impression that we wish to
hold Austria back. The case is solely one of finding a way to realize Austria's
desired aim, that of cutting the vital cord of the Greater-Serbia propaganda,   15
without at the same time bringing on a world war, and, if the latter cannot be
avoided in the end, of improving the conditions under which we shall have to
wage it, in so far as is possible.

L. L. Snyder, *Documents of German History*, pp. 330–1

Questions

1   How do you account for the Kaiser's responses (a) to Grey's suggestion
of a conference [5.25] on 25 July and (b) to the Austrian reply to the
ultimatum on 28 July?
2   How seriously did Bethmann Hollweg seek to restrain Austria in [5.26]?
3   Compare the Kaiser's and Bethmann Hollweg's reactions to the Serbian
reply to the ultimatum.

After the Austrian declaration of war on Serbia all eyes now turned to St
Petersburg. Having decided on 24 July to support Serbia the Russian government felt obliged to go to a state of partial mobilisation as soon as it heard
of the Austrian declaration of war (28 July). Pressed by his ministers because
of the impracticability of such half measures, the Tsar consented to full
mobilisation on 29 July. That evening, on receipt of a conciliatory letter from
Wilhelm II, he revoked that decision, but at 3.00 p.m. on 30 July he was
finally persuaded by Sazonoff to order full mobilisation. It came into effect
on 31 July. The German response was immediately to suspend the last-

minute initiative which Bethmann Hollweg had been ready to launch on 30 July [5.27] and to deliver an ultimatum on 31 July requiring Russia to cease all military measures against Germany and Austria within twelve hours. When no reply was received at 5.00 p.m. on 1 August Germany declared war.

The remorseless logic of the Schlieffen plan now came into play. Though Germany had no direct quarrel with France, that country must be defeated first, and that could only be achieved through the violation of Belgian neutrality. There was no hesitation in military circles over what needed to be done. Excuses were found for a declaration of war on France on 3 August and, after the Belgian rejection of an ultimatum demanding the unopposed passage of German troops, the Belgian frontier was crossed in the early hours of 4 August.

5.27–28 throw light on German responsibility for the transformation of the Austro-Serbian conflict into the First World War. The first document contains the instructions Bethmann Hollweg prepared to send to Tschirschky on the night of 30 July. By this time he was aware that he could not count on British neutrality in the event of war with France. Before the telegram could be delivered news came through at about 11.00 p.m. of Russian mobilisation. These instructions were immediately cancelled.

5.27 Telegram from Bethmann Hollweg to Tschirschky, 9.00 p.m. 30 July

If Vienna, as appears probable ... rejects any mediation in particular Grey's latest proposal, it is hardly possible any longer to put the blame for the European conflagration on Russia ... If Britain is successful in these attempts [to halt Russian and French military measures] while Vienna rejects everything, Vienna shows that it is determined to have a war into which we are drawn while Russia   5 remains free from guilt. For us this creates a totally unacceptable situation as regards our own nation. We can therefore only urge Austria to accept Grey's proposal [of mediation] which safeguards its position in every respect.

F. Fischer, *War of Illusions*, pp. 497–8

5.28 Sir Edward Goschen, British ambassador in Berlin, describes German justification for the invasion of Belgium in interviews held with Jagow (foreign secretary) and Bethmann Hollweg on 4 August

Herr von Jagow again went into the reasons why the Imperial Government had been obliged to take this step – namely that they had to advance into France by the quickest and easiest road – so as to be able to get well ahead with their operations and endeavour to strike some decisive blow as early as possible.

I found the Chancellor very agitated. His Excellency at once began a harangue   5
which lasted for twenty minutes. He said that the step taken by His Majesty's
Government was terrible to a degree, just for a word 'neutrality', a word which in
wartime had often been disregarded – just for a scrap of paper [the treaty
guaranteeing Belgian neutrality, signed among others by Britain and Prussia in
1838].

L. L. Snyder, *Documents of German History*, pp. 332–3

The final document contains passages from the Lichnowsky Memorandum,
written in 1915 by the man who was German ambassador in London from
1912 to 1914. Anglophile in his sympathies, his Memorandum was thought
to be too critical of German policy when it was first published in 1927 and
various passages were cut. The original document was discovered by Röhl in
1967 and the passages reproduced are among those that were censored in
1927.

5.29   The Lichnowsky Memorandum (unexpurgated edition)

Either we wanted war as a preventive measure – and the Reich Chancellor is said
to have given the Austrians to understand that this was the case – or we seriously
misjudged the consequences of our policy when we handed our entire army over
to Count Berchtold for the Serbian affair. I ask: is it a peaceful policy to urge a
war which contains at least the probability of world conflagration? We allegedly   5
wanted peace, but only on condition that Russia would give her blessing to the
annihilation of Serbia in the name of the monarchic principle ...
  On our side nothing, absolutely nothing, was done to preserve peace, and
when we at last decided to do what I had advocated from the first, it was too
late. By then Russia, as a result of our harsh attitude and that of Count   10
Berchtold, had lost all confidence and mobilised. The war party gained the upper
hand.

J. C. G. Röhl, *1914: Delusion or Design*, pp. 101–4

Questions

1   How do you account for the Kaiser's rejection of mediation by Grey on
    25 July and Bethmann Hollweg's support for it on 30 July [5.25, 5.27]?
2   What light does 5.28 throw on Bethmann Hollweg's attitude to the out-
    break of the First World War?
3   How far do 5.22–5.28 support Lichnowsky's verdict that 'on our side
    nothing, absolutely nothing, was done to preserve peace ...' [5.29]?

6 Germany and the First World War

The First World War brought about Germany's defeat and the collapse of the empire inaugurated in 1871. The two disasters were inextricably linked, and to the neutral observer it might seem poetic justice that an empire created by the sword should also perish by the sword. There was, however, nothing inevitable about the scale or manner of Germany's defeat; nor was it beyond the realm of possibility that the imperial regime might have been successfully transformed into a constitutional monarchy, as for a brief moment it was in the last days of October 1918.

It is the purpose of this final chapter to examine some of the reasons for the disastrous outcome that actually materialised. Granted the initial disparity between the Central Powers (Germany, Austria and Turkey, later joined by Bulgaria) and the *Entente* Powers (Russia, France and Britain, later joined by Japan, Italy, Rumania and the United States) it might seem that the prospect of a German victory was always remote. But with the collapse of the eastern front following the outbreak of the Russian revolution and the initial success of the unrestricted U-boat campaign, both in the spring of 1917, victory looked increasingly possible. In March 1918 Germany was able to impose the draconian peace of Brest-Litovsk on Russia and at the same time launch the most threatening offensive since the Schlieffen plan on the western front. The announcement of unrestricted U-boat warfare, coupled with the Zimmermann telegram, brought the United States into the war, however, and this almost certainly turned the scales to Germany's disadvantage. The first part of the chapter examines the strategic choices made in 1917 and 1918 which culminated in Germany's defeat [6.1–6.8].

If victory proved unattainable then Germany's fate depended on whether a compromise peace could be reached. This in turn hinged on the nature of German ambitions. The greater these were, the less the chance of a negotiated peace and an early end to the war. The second part of this chapter is devoted to an analysis of German war aims, which fluctuated with Germany's military fortunes [6.9–6.15].

Finally, it is necessary to explain why defeat led to the Kaiser's abdication and the treaty of Versailles. At the outset of the war Germany was united as she had never been before. The Kaiser proclaimed a *Burgfrieden*, a civil peace, with the words 'I no longer recognize parties, I recognize only Germans' (Craig, *Germany, 1866–1945*, p. 340). The Social Democrats, whom he had so castigated, voted for War Credits for the duration of the war, and the Catholic Centre Party joined the coalition in the Reichstag which generally supported the chancellor. Yet by 1917 a polarisation of political parties had taken effect. On the left, the Independent Social Democratic Party broke away from the SPD in April 1917, and was itself outflanked by the Spartacus League which had been formed in 1916 by Rosa Luxemburg and others. On the right, Admiral Tirpitz and some fellow conservatives formed the Fatherland Party in September 1917 to promote a more aggressive prosecution of the war. Belated attempts to bring about political reform in the spring of 1917 came to nothing and, with Bethmann Hollweg's resignation in July 1917, the direction of policy passed into the hands of the military duo, Hindenburg and Ludendorff. The combination of grandiose and unrealistic ambition coupled with obstinate refusal to contemplate political reform meant that when defeat came there was no support for the regime which had brought it about [**6.16–6.26**].

German war strategy

The war developed in ways which no one anticipated. Once the Schlieffen plan had failed, as it did by the middle of September 1914, Germany, like all the other powers, was sucked into a war of attrition whose outcome would be decided as much by resources as by the fighting capacity of the combatants. In such a contest the Central Powers were at a serious disadvantage. In 1914 Germany depended on imports for over a third of her foodstuffs and for much of her strategic raw materials such as nitrates. In terms of manpower the *Entente* powers with a combined population from Britain, France, Italy and Russia of 230 million easily outnumbered the populations of Germany and Austria-Hungary (115 million). The Central Powers enjoyed the advantage of fighting on interior lines, but they had to face war on several different fronts simultaneously. The British navy soon established a blockade of Germany's coastline which closed all German ports, and by 1917 had effectively prevented German imports through neighbouring neutral states such as Sweden and Holland. It has been calculated that 700,000 German civilians died as a result of malnutrition as well as the 2.5 million servicemen who died on active service.

These disadvantages did not however deter the military cliques who ultimately determined policy and it has to be said that Germany's capacity to
make war was barely affected by the shortage of resources or manpower until
1918. In fact, to some observers a German victory looked as likely in 1917 as
it had ever done. By this time the western front had become a vast killing
field in which neither side could claim an advantage. British and French
offensives in 1915 and 1916 had been successfully, if expensively, repulsed.
Equally, the German attempts to break through at Ypres in 1914 and 1915
had failed, as had the long-drawn-out assault on Verdun in 1916.

On the eastern front, on the other hand, a German victory was in
prospect. After the battles of Tannenberg and the Masurian lakes in August
1914 Germany was able to occupy Courland and Estonia and much of
Poland. Brusilov's successful offensive against Austria-Hungary in Galicia in
1916 was more than counterbalanced by the German defeat of Rumania.
Serbia had been occupied in 1915. Internal disaffection was beginning to
affect the Russian war effort.

At sea, while the German imperial navy had inflicted greater casualties
than it sustained at the battle of Jutland in May 1916, it had failed to break
British naval superiority, and was unwilling to renew the challenge. The
odds were thus evenly balanced. With the impending collapse of Russia, if
Britain could be starved into surrender and the stalemate broken on the
western front a German victory still looked possible. It was these considerations that determined German war strategy in 1917 and 1918.

The decision to adopt unrestricted U-boat warfare

At the outset of the war Germany had twenty-one submarines. Tirpitz had
always envisaged the struggle for naval supremacy being fought by rival
battle fleets. But Bethmann Hollweg was always reluctant to risk using the
German navy in such a role. Should it be lost, Germany would have forfeited a valuable bargaining counter in the peace negotiations that must at some
point bring the war to an end. After the battle of Jutland the German fleet
stayed in the harbour, apart from an occasional brief foray. If Germany was
to combat the British naval blockade an alternative was needed and the submarine appeared to be the answer. For the first three years of the war only
seven U-boats were lost to enemy action and the toll on merchant shipping
rose steadily. Pressure to adopt unrestricted U-boat warfare mounted.

But the decision to do so was taken only after much hesitation and several
false starts for the arguments were evenly balanced. Against the prospect
of starving Britain, dependent for one third of her foodstuffs on imports,

into surrender was the risk that the policy would not be effective and would damage German relations with neutral powers, most notably the United States. Moral considerations did not enter the equation for German public opinion saw no difference between Britain's blockade, in which wheat was contraband, and the use of U-boats to deny food to British consumers [6.1]. Opinion in Germany was sharply divided, however, on the wisdom of a U-boat campaign. The first step was taken on 4 February 1915 when all the waters round Britain were declared a war zone in which any merchant vessel might be sunk. The sinking of the *Lusitania* on 7 May, with the loss of 1,200 lives, including those of 128 Americans, brought a reappraisal of the policy and by September 1915 German submarines had been ordered to suspend their attacks on neutral and passenger shipping.

A further determined effort to renew the submarine campaign was made by Admiral Tirpitz and Falkenhayn, chief of the General Staff, in the spring of 1916 [6.2]. On this occasion Bethmann Hollweg successfully held off the challenge, with the Kaiser's approval, and Tirpitz shortly after resigned [6.3(a)]. His successor, Admiral Henning von Holtzendorff, was no less enthusiastic about the prospects of unrestricted U-boat warfare, and in a memorandum which he produced for the Kaiser in January 1917 argued that if 600,000 tons of shipping could be sunk each month, a perfectly feasible target in his view, Britain would be forced to surrender within five months. This time Bethmann Hollweg gave way [6.3(b)] and on 9 January 1917 an imperial council resolved on a policy of unrestricted U-boat warfare to be announced on 31 January.

When this happened American opinion was duly outraged, but it was still two months before the United States entered the war. President Wilson failed to get through Congress a measure authorising the arming of US merchant ships and had to do it by executive order instead. However, his task was eased by the telegram sent to the German ambassador in Mexico by the German foreign secretary, Arthur Zimmermann [6.4]. The telegram instructed the German ambassador to offer assistance to Mexico, should war break out between Germany and the United States. It was intercepted by British naval intelligence and published in the United States on 1 March 1917. It may not, by itself, have been instrumental in bringing America into the war, but it meant that Wilson had comfortable majorities in both houses of Congress when on 2 April he sought their approval for his war message. How much difference this would make to Germany no one could predict. At the time the U-boat campaign appeared to be working. In April 1917, 373 ships were sunk, 869,103 tons in total. British counter-measures, notably the use of convoys, soon had a marked effect however, and in the rest of 1917 of

26,604 vessels convoyed only 147 (0.55%) were lost. In the same period 65 U-boats out of an operational total of 139 were lost. The following documents illustrate the debate on this critical issue.

6.1 Bethmann Hollweg's reservations, January 1915

Measures like a submarine blockade, which are certain to have a negative effect on the attitude of the neutrals and our supplies, can only be undertaken when our military situation is so secure that the issue is beyond doubt and the danger of the neutrals joining our enemies can be ruled out.

K. H. Jarausch, *The Enigmatic Chancellor*, p. 281

6.2 A memorandum from Admiral Tirpitz, February 1916

Immediate and relentless recourse to the submarine weapon is absolutely necessary. Any further delay in the introduction of unrestricted warfare will give England time for further naval and economic measures, cause us greater losses in the end, and endanger quick success. The sooner the campaign be opened, the sooner will success be realised, and the more rapidly and energetically will   5
England's hope of defeating us by a war of exhaustion be destroyed. If we defeat England, we break the backbone of the hostile coalition.

Alfred von Tirpitz, *My Memoirs*, vol. 2, p. 419

6.3(a) Kurt Riezler, his private secretary, describes Bethmann Hollweg's successful opposition to unrestricted U-boat warfare, March 1916

On the eve of the crucial decision Bethmann 'was very nervous, smoked countless cigarettes, moved from chair to chair, but was also firmly resolved to avoid a rupture with America and equally determined to leave his office if the decision was negative.' In Charleville, to his pleasant surprise, 'the emperor said ... that he completely endorsed [his] memorandum and did not think of risking war with   5
America – the chancellor should not be afraid, he would tell the others that.'

K. H. Jarausch, *The Enigmatic Chancellor*, p. 284

6.3(b) Bethmann Hollweg acquiesces in the decision to adopt unrestricted U-boat warfare, 9 January 1917

When the military authorities consider submarine warfare essential, I am not in a position to object.

K. H. Jarausch, *The Enigmatic Chancellor*, p. 300

6.4   The Zimmermann telegram to the German ambassador in Mexico as it was published to the American public, 1 March 1917

We intend to begin unrestricted submarine warfare on the first day of February. We shall endeavour in spite of this to keep the United States neutral. In the event of this not succeeding, we make Mexico a proposal of alliance on the following basis: Make war together, generous financial support, and an understanding on our part that Mexico is to reconquer the lost territory in Texas,   5 New Mexico and Arizona. The settlement in detail is left up to you.

R. B. Asprey, *The German High Command at War*, **p. 300**

Questions

1   Summarise the arguments for and against unrestricted U-boat warfare as they are presented in **6.1** and **6.2**.
2   Why was Bethmann Hollweg successful in 1916 but unsuccessful in 1917 in resisting the demand for unrestricted U-boat warfare [**6.3**]?
3   Assess the importance of the Zimmermann telegram [**6.4**] in bringing the United States into the war.

Germany's final offensive and collapse on the western front

If the U-boat campaign failed to live up to the promise of its advocates, the *Entente*'s hopes of victory in 1917 were similarly dashed. In April General Nivelle launched what proved to be a disastrous French offensive on well-prepared German positions whose only result was a wave of mutinies in fifty-five French units. The danger of a collapse in French morale and the British admiralty's insistence that the capture of German U-boat bases at Ostend and Zeebrugge was of critical importance lent support to Haig's ambitious plans for an offensive in Flanders, despite Lloyd George's well-founded suspicions. The battle of Passchendaele, as it came to be called, lasting from 31 July to 15 November, achieved derisory gains at enormous costs to the British army.

With the signing of the treaty of Brest-Litovsk on 3 March 1918 Ludendorff was now in a position to deliver what he hoped would be the clinching blow on the western front. Such an offensive had been envisaged at a conference held at Mons on 11 November 1917 though what precisely Ludendorff hoped to achieve by it was far from clear [**6.5**]. The Kaiser, still sanguine, evidently hoped to be able to dictate peace terms [**6.6**].

6.5 Ludendorff justifies the 1918 offensive in his memoirs

The army had come victoriously through 1917; but it had become apparent that the holding of the western front could no longer be counted on, in view of the enormous quantity of material of all kinds which the *Entente* had at their disposal ... Against the weight of the enemy's material the troops no longer displayed their old stubbornness; they thought with horror of fresh defensive battles and longed for a war of movement. 5

C. Barnett, *The Swordbearers*, p. 280

6.6 Marginal note by Wilhelm II, recorded in Admiral Müller's diary, January 1918

The victory of the Germans over Russia was the pre-condition for the revolution, which was the pre-condition for Lenin, who was the pre-condition for Brest! The same applies in the west! First victory in the west and collapse of the Entente, then we shall make conditions which they have to accept! And they will be framed purely in accordance with our interests.

F. Fischer, *Germany's Aims in the First World War*, p. 610

At the very moment when the offensive was being planned President Wilson announced his Fourteen Points to Congress (4 January 1918). So far as Germany was concerned they required the evacuation of Belgium, the evacuation of all Russian territory, the return to France of Alsace-Lorraine and the setting up of an independent Poland. In his reply of 24 January Hertling, German chancellor from October 1917 to October 1918, rejected any intervention by Wilson in the future of the territories occupied by Germany and any cession of German territory in the east or west. The decision to go for victory ended the last opportunity of a negotiated peace and condemned Germany to much worse terms than she might have obtained had the March offensive never been launched.

It began with operation Michael on 21 March and continued with varying success until 22 July. How close it came to succeeding is hard to judge. At one point the Germans were within fifty miles of Paris and were on the point of splitting the French and British armies. On 9 April Haig issued his famous order 'With our backs to the wall and believing in the justice of our cause each man must fight to the end'. But there were signs of indiscipline in the German armies as they overran enemy positions and enjoyed the plentiful rations they were able to seize. The pace of the German advance outstripped the capacity of the outworn transport system to maintain supplies. As soon as the *Entente* launched its counter attacks many German soldiers preferred to surrender rather than continue the fight. On 8 August, 'the black day of the German army', according to Ludendorff, the Germans lost 27,000 men, two-thirds of whom surrendered.

On 28 September Ludendorff, who had suffered a psychological collapse himself, called on Hindenburg to request an immediate armistice. The following day, together with the new foreign secretary, Paul von Hintze, they requested the Kaiser to form a new government and to open negotiations with President Wilson. On 1 October Ludendorff informed his staff that an armistice was being sought. In view of the legend that Germany was 'stabbed in the back' by weak-willed politicians rather than defeated at the front, the view of Prince Rupprecht of Bavaria, one of Germany's more able generals, and Ludendorff's own testimony are important [6.7, 6.8].

6.7 Prince Rupprecht of Bavaria advises against an offensive

We are indeed in a position to strike a few powerful blows at the enemy in the west but scarcely to bring on a decisive defeat, thus it is to be expected that the battle within a few months will once again become a tedious war of position. Who will finally win depends above all on who is able to make do the longest with his effective manpower, and in this respect I am convinced that the enemy   5
is better off, thanks to the Americans, who of course have become effective only gradually.

R. B. Asprey, *The German High Command*, **p. 364**

6.8 Ludendorff's demand for an armistice, 1 October 1918

I can hold the troops today, but I cannot foretell what will happen tomorrow ... The army cannot wait another forty-eight hours, a breakthrough with disastrous consequences is possible at any moment.

R. B. Asprey, *The German High Command*, **p. 470**

Questions

1   Contrast the reasons given for the March offensive by Ludendorff and the Kaiser [6.5, 6.6].
2   In the light of 6.4 and 6.7 how justified was Ludendorff's decision to launch the March 1918 offensive?
3   How comprehensively was Germany defeated on the western front?

German war aims

'By a curious reversal the idealism of self-defense turned into lust for conquest' (Jarausch, *The Enigmatic Chancellor*, p. 186). There can be little doubt that the impression Bethmann Hollweg wished to convey to the Reichstag on 4 August 1914 was that Germany had been forced into a defensive war [6.9]. But from the outset there were strong pressures on him to use the war to extend Germany's frontiers to the east, the west and in Africa. The Pan-German League wanted the economic and political domination of *Mitteleuropa* [6.10]. The military authorities demanded the acquisition of Russia's Baltic provinces and a frontier strip of Poland to give Germany secure frontiers in the east, and the occupation of Belgium to protect Germany in the west. Industrialists, anxious to make Germany self-sufficient in iron ore, pressed for the annexation of the Longwy Brieu iron and coal basin in western France. The German colonial secretary, Wilhelm Solf, aimed at the consolidation of a German Central African colonial empire through the acquisition of French, Belgian, Portuguese and possibly British colonies. How far Bethmann Hollweg shared these ambitions, or merely acquiesced in them, is open to question. He evidently supported at least some of them in the September programme drafted by his secretary, Kurt Riezler, in September 1914, when a swift German victory looked possible [6.11]. Later in the war he accepted what came to be known as the Kreuznach programme, drawn up in its essentials by the German High Command in April 1917, though adding to it his own reservations [6.12].

In contrast to these ambitions there was a growing body of opinion which favoured a peace without annexations or indemnities, particularly as the war progressed. Initially it had few supporters, but by 1917 a large number of Reichstag deputies were prepared to support it. In July 1917 Matthias Erzberger of the Centre Party introduced a Peace Resolution which was passed by 212 votes to 126, the majority being made up of members of the Centre, Progressive and Social Democratic Parties [6.13(a)]. Unfortunately its impact was blunted by the removal of Bethmann Hollweg. The new chancellor, Georg Michaelis, added a saving clause 'As I understand them' both to the Peace Resolution and the government's acceptance of it and in a note to the crown prince on 25 July made clear how little effect the Peace Resolution would have on German policy [6.13(b)].

With Bethmann Hollweg's resignation in July 1917 the last significant brake on the annexationists disappeared and the collapse of Russia in revolution only whetted their appetites. Rather than seeking an accommodation with the provisional government established in Russia in March 1917, the German foreign office preferred to promote the further disintegration of

Russia by supporting the Bolsheviks [6.14]. When negotiating with Lenin in January 1918 Germany drove a very hard bargain. The full extent of German ambitions was concealed in the wording of the treaty of Brest-Litovsk, which paid lip-service to the principle of self-determination. In practice Germany sought the political and economic domination of all the areas which Russia surrendered [6.15(a), (b)]. The following documents give some indication of German war aims as they were both privately and publicly expressed.

6.9   Speech by Bethmann Hollweg to the Reichstag, 4 August 1914

A stupendous fate is breaking over Europe. For forty-four years, since the time when we fought for and won the German Empire and our position in the world, we have lived in peace and have protected the peace of Europe. In the works of peace we have become strong and powerful, and have thus aroused the envy of others. With patience we have faced the fact that, under the pretense that   5
Germany was desirous of war, enmity has been awakened against us in the East and in the West, and chains have been fashioned for us. The wind then sown has brought forth the whirlwind which has now broken loose. We wished to continue our work of peace, and, like a silent vow, the feeling that animated everyone from the Emperor down to the youngest soldier was this: Only in defense of a just   10
cause shall our sword fly from its scabbard.

The day has now come when we must draw it, against our wish, and in spite of our sincere endeavours. Russia has set fire to the building. We are at war with Russia and France – a war that has been forced upon us.

L. L. Snyder, *Documents of German History*, p. 338

6.10   Memorandum on German war aims produced by the Executive Committee of the Pan-German League on 28 August 1914

It is an absolutely imperative demand, and widely accepted as such, that Mitteleuropa, inclusive of those areas to be acquired by the German Reich and Austria-Hungary as prizes of victory, must form one great united economic unit. The Netherlands and Switzerland, the three Scandinavian States and Finland, Italy, Rumania and Bulgaria will attach themselves to this nucleus gradually and   5
of compulsive necessity, without the need of the least pressure from the nucleus-States. If one includes the dependencies of these States, the result will be a vast economic unit capable of asserting and maintaining its economic-political independence against any other in the world.

F. Fischer, *Germany's Aims in the First World War*, p. 106

6.11   The September programme – 'a preliminary note on the guidelines of our policy at the conclusion of peace which I [Bethmann Hollweg] have had prepared here' (9 September 1914)

The 'general aim of the war' was, for him [Bethmann Hollweg], 'security for the German Reich in west and east for all imaginable time. For this purpose France must be so weakened as to make her revival as a great power impossible for all time. Russia must be thrust back as far as possible from Germany's eastern frontier and her domination over the non-Russian vassal peoples broken.'   5

The 'individual war aims' were confined for the time being to the west, where alone the conclusion of peace seemed within grasp. They included:

1. *France* The military to decide whether we should demand cession of Belfort and western slopes of the Vosges, razing of fortresses and cession of coastal strip from Dunkirk to Boulogne.   10

The ore-field of Briey, which is necessary for our industry, to be ceded in any case.

Further a war indemnity, to be paid in instalments; it must be high enough to prevent France from spending any considerable sums on armaments in the next 15–20 years ...   15

2. *Belgium* Liège and Verviers to be attached to Prussia, a frontier strip of the province of Luxemburg to Luxemburg.

Question whether Antwerp, with a corridor to Liège, should also be annexed remains open.

At any rate Belgium, even if allowed to continue to exist as a state, must be   20
reduced to a vassal state, must allow us to occupy any militarily important ports, must place her coast at our disposal in military respects, must become economically a German province ...

3. *Luxemburg.* Will become a German federal state.

4. We must create a *central European economic association* through common   25
customs treaties, to include France, Belgium, Holland, Denmark, Austria-Hungary, Poland [sic], and perhaps Italy, Sweden and Norway. This association will not have any supreme constitutional authority and all its members will be formally equal, but in practice will be under German leadership and must stabilise Germany's economic dominance over Mitteleuropa.   30

5. *The question of colonial acquisitions*, where the first aim is the creation of a continuous Central African colonial empire will be considered later, as will that of the aims to be realised *vis-à-vis* Russia.

F. Fischer, *Germany's Aims in the First World War*, p. 104

Questions

1   Why, and with what justification, did Bethmann Hollweg claim in **6.9** to be fighting 'a war that has been forced on us'?
2   To what extent do **6.10** and **6.11** contradict the claim that 'only in a just cause shall our sword fly from its scabbard' [**6.9, lines 10–11**]?
3   How far can **6.10** and **6.11** be seen as an accurate reflection of German war aims?

With the outbreak of the Russian revolution in March 1917, Bethmann Hollweg saw an opportunity of splitting the *Entente*. But at the Kreuznach conference held in April, the military high command with the Kaiser's support succeeded in imposing their tough demands on an unwilling chancellor. There was little change to the September programme so far as the west was concerned, but in the east the Kreuznach protocol included the following specific requirements:

6.12   The Kreuznach Protocol

1. Estonia and Lithuania must be won for the German Empire up to the line indicated by OHL [*Oberste Heeresleitung*, Supreme Army Command].
2. The delineation of the German border towards Poland depends upon the future relationship of Poland to the empire [but should include the Narev line and the Germanization of a border strip] ...   5
    Bethmann Hollweg added an emphatic reservation to the record: 'I consider the agreed peace conditions attainable only if we can *dictate* the peace. Solely under this precondition have I assented.'

K. H. Jarausch, *The Enigmatic Chancellor*, **pp. 223–4**

In contrast to the Kreuznach programme, the moderate parties in the Reichstag, less sanguine than OHL about the prospects of victory, supported the Peace Resolution that was introduced by Matthias Erzberger in July 1917:

6.13(a)   The Peace Resolution, 19 July 1917

The Reichstag seeks a peace of understanding and a lasting reconciliation among peoples. Any violations of territory and political, economic and financial oppression are incompatible with such a peace ...
    However, as long as the enemy governments disassociate themselves from such a peace, as long as they threaten Germany and her allies with conquest and   5

domination, then so long shall the German people stand united and unshaken, and will fight until their right and the right of their allies to live and grow is made secure.

L. L. Snyder, *Documents of German History,* **p. 362**

The passage of the Peace Resolution secured the continued support of the SPD and Centre Party in financing the German war effort but its effect on German war aims can perhaps be gauged by a letter which the new German chancellor, Michaelis, wrote to the crown prince on 25 July 1917:

6.13(b)

I have deprived it [the Peace Resolution] of its most dangerous features by my interpretation of it (italics in the original). 'One can make any peace one likes with this resolution'.

F. Fischer, *Germany's Aims in the First World War,* **p. 404**

This rapidly became apparent in the German response to the Russian Revolution which opened up the possibility of a compromise peace. Instead of seeking an accommodation with the provisional government the German foreign office adopted the policy urged by its head of mission in Denmark, Count Ulrich von Brockdorff-Rantzau, later to be the first foreign secretary in the Weimar Republic. Brockdorff-Rantzau had long advocated supporting revolution in Russia as a way of ending the Tsarist regime. Now he advised a policy designed to bring about chaos:

6.14   Memorandum to the German foreign office from Count Ulrich Brockdorff-Rantzau, 2 April 1917

We must now unconditionally seek to create in Russia the greatest possible chaos ... We should do all we can ... to exacerbate the differences between the moderate and the extremist parties, because we have the greatest interest in the latter gaining the upper hand, since the Revolution will then become unavoidable and assume forms that must shatter the stability of the Russian state.

R. Pipes, *The Russian Revolution,* **p. 390**

Similar advice came from the German envoy in Switzerland, and in consequence arrangements were made for Lenin to travel across Germany to Sweden in a sealed train, and thence to St Petersburg. The Treasury also approved expenditure of five million marks to aid the revolution. In the short term the gambit proved astonishingly successful. With Lenin's triumph and his determination to withdraw from the war, Germany was now in a strong position. Between November 1917 and March 1918 there ensued a prolonged diplomatic battle between the German government and the Bolsheviks. On 22 November Lenin issued his Decree on peace calling for a three-month armistice and a peace without annexations or reparations. Germany responded rapidly and on 3 December armistice talks began at Brest-Litovsk. They led to the official opening of negotiations on 27 December. German intentions were initially concealed by their apparent acceptance of Lenin's formula, but it soon became clear that Germany expected the cession of those areas which she occupied, notably Courland, Lithuania and parts of Poland, as well as a separate peace treaty with the Ukraine. These demands were made quite explicit on 18 January and led to the withdrawal of the Russian delegation, led by Trotsky, who on 10 February declared a state of 'no war, no peace' and left Brest-Litovsk. On 18 February Germany renewed hostilities and advanced further into Russia. On 21 February an ultimatum was delivered by the German government calling for immediate acceptance of the German terms. Refusal would be met by an advance on St Petersburg. Following a stormy debate in the Central Executive Committee of the Bolshevik Party, Lenin secured a narrow majority for acceptance, by 116 votes to 85, with 26 abstentions. On 3 March 1918 the Treaty of Brest-Litovsk was signed. While lip service was paid to the wishes of the inhabitants of the territories Russia was to evacuate, in practice the treaty meant a huge increase in German territorial power. When the treaty was presented to the Reichstag it was approved by all the right wing and moderate parties. The SPD abstained. Only the Independent Socialists voted against it. Documents **6.15(a)** and **6.15(b)** list some of the key terms of the treaty and the interpretation placed on them by the German foreign secretary at the time, Richard von Kühlmann.

6.15(a)   The Treaty of Brest-Litovsk (selected terms), 3 March 1918

ARTICLE III. The territories lying to the west of the line agreed upon by the contracting parties which formerly belonged to Russia, will no longer be subject to Russian sovereignty; the line agreed upon is traced on the map submitted as an essential part of the treaty of peace. The exact fixation of the line will be established by a Russo-German commission ...   5

   Russia refrains from all interference in the internal relations of these territories. Germany and Austria-Hungary propose to determine the future status of these territories in agreement with their population.

ARTICLE VI. Russia obligates herself to conclude peace at once with the Ukrainian People's Republic and to recognize the treaty of peace between the   10 state and the powers of the Quadruple Alliance [i.e. the Central powers]. The Ukrainian territory will, without delay, be cleared of Russian troops and the Russian Red Guard ...

Esthonia and Livonia will likewise, without delay, be cleared of Russian troops and the Russian Red Guard ... Esthonia and Livonia will be occupied by a   15 German police force until security is insured by proper national institutions and until public order has been established.

L. L. Snyder, *Documents of German History*, pp. 364–5

6.15(b)   Richard von Kühlmann explains his strategy at Brest-Litovsk in his memoirs, published in 1948

My plan was to entangle Trotsky in a purely academic discussion on the right of self-determination and the possibility of applying it in practice, and to get for ourselves through the right of national self-determination whatever territorial concessions we absolutely needed.

F. Fischer, *Germany's Aims in the First World War*, p. 479

Questions

1   On what grounds did OHL demand the cession of Estonia, Lithuania and part of Poland in the Kreuznach protocol **[6.12]**?
2   How significant a modification to the September Programme was the Peace Resolution of July 1917 **[6.11, 6.13(a), (b)]**?
3   How far was the advice given in **6.14** adopted?
4   Does **6.15(b)** completely invalidate the promise made in **6.15(a), lines** 7–8 'to determine the future status of these territories in agreement with their population'?
5   In view of the Peace Resolution of July 1917, how do you account for the lack of opposition to the treaty of Brest-Litovsk in the Reichstag in 1918?

The collapse of the empire

With Germany's defeat came the collapse of the empire, the Kaiser abdicating on 9 November 1918, two days before the armistice was signed. Three possible explanations are examined in the final section of this chapter: the shift to the right in the direction of policy; the failure of reform; and the polarisation of political parties and opinions which resulted in the complete breakdown of support for the old regime.

The direction of policy

There was no change in the institutional structure of the empire during the war, and the same weaknesses evident in peacetime were if anything exacerbated by the strains of warfare. Wilhelm's position should in theory have been strengthened by the right of command (the *Kommandogewalt*) which the constitution conferred on him. He was now able to perform the role of supreme warlord in earnest, instead of merely playing at it as he had done on manoeuvres. It was Wilhelm's tragedy, as it was Germany's, that he was neither intellectually nor emotionally equipped for the part. While the ultimate power of decision rested with him, he had no clear grasp of strategic or political realities and swung between moods of euphoria and despair with equal rapidity. Like all weak men, he was open to persuasion by those more strong minded than himself. By 1917 he had effectively been sidelined, as he himself realised [6.16].

If Wilhelm was not to be the director of policy this left the chancellor in apparent control. But Bethmann Hollweg was constrained by the need to retain the Kaiser's confidence, the support of the military and the approval of the Reichstag in any initiative he might take. Bethmann Hollweg described his course as a diagonal, steering between the rival forces of left and right, in an attempt to keep the ship of state on an even keel. As we shall see, this proved an impossible task. In theory the Reichstag elected in 1912 should have been a moderating influence. Between them the moderate and left-wing parties, the Centre, Progressive and Social Democratic Parties, commanded a comfortable majority – 243 seats out of 397. In practice such a coalition rarely materialised and when it did, as in the Peace Resolution of 1917, the Reichstag had no way of making its wishes effective. Furthermore Bethmann Hollweg failed to establish a working relationship with this group for fear of antagonising the right.

As the war progressed, power shifted inexorably into the hands of the military. Ironically it was Bethmann Hollweg who started the process. In August 1916 he urged the replacement of Erich von Falkenhayn by the duo of Hindenburg and Ludendorff. Their victories on the eastern front stood in sharp contrast to the German failure to take Verdun which Falkenhayn had made the centrepiece of his strategy on the western front. Somewhat against his better judgement, Wilhelm accepted his chancellor's advice. At the time, Hindenburg was sixty-nine and was little more than a massive and reassuring presence. Ludendorff was fifty-one, a brilliant staff officer and a man of powerful patriotic convictions. Hindenburg was given the title of Chief of the General Staff, Ludendorff that of First Quartermaster General, but Ludendorff was to share command responsibility 'in all decisions and measures that might be taken' (Asprey, *The German High Command*, p. 252). In view of the disparity in their ages and abilities, it was Ludendorff who now became the dominating influence on German policy. Though there was no formal reallocation of responsibilities, through the myth of their indispensability, sedulously cultivated, both Hindenburg and Ludendorff were now invulnerable and hence became the chief influence on policy.

Nowhere is this better illustrated than in the steps leading to Bethmann Hollweg's own resignation in July 1917. By this stage the duo had lost all confidence in the chancellor, both because of the domestic reforms he had initiated in the spring of 1917 (see pp. 132–3) and because of his belief in the need for a negotiated peace. Through Colonel Bauer, a henchman of Ludendorff's, a campaign to get rid of Bethmann Hollweg was orchestrated in the Reichstag. On July 9, Stresemann, leader of the National Liberals, and Erzberger, leader of the Centre Party, called for his resignation. At the same time Hindenburg and Ludendorff threatened to resign if Bethmann Hollweg was not removed. Faced with these pressures, Bethmann Hollweg took what he believed the only honourable course open to him, and resigned on 13 July. Publicly, he blamed his failure on his relations with the Reichstag. In private audience he acknowledged the blackmail tactics of Hindenburg and Ludendorff [6.17].

With his resignation the coast was clear for Ludendorff, through Hindenburg, to take over the direction of German war strategy. The new chancellor, Georg Michaelis, a little-known civil servant, lasted only until October. His replacement, Count Georg von Hertling was no cipher but, a Bavarian elder-statesman like Caprivi, he had neither the energy nor the strength to reassert the chancellor's authority. These changes in the power structure are illustrated in **6.16** and **6.17**.

6.16   The Kaiser reflects on his position (undated)

If Germany believes that I lead the army, it is mistaken. I drink tea and cut wood, go for walks, and then find out from time to time what has been decided, just as the generals please.

K. H. Jarausch, *The Enigmatic Chancellor*, p. 265

6.17   Bethmann Hollweg's resignation

Amidst this frantic confusion, Bethmann decided on the ultimate self-sacrifice: 'I said to H.M. [the Kaiser]: "Of course the resignation of Hindenburg and Ludendorff is out of the question" and took my leave.' ... After a soul-searching

discussion with Valentini [chief of the civil cabinet], the chancellor drafted his
letter of resignation on the morning of July 13: 'The general situation of the   5
Reichstag has, as I cannot deny, developed in such a manner that a future
solution can only be achieved if Y.M. has the grace to relieve me of my office.'

K. H. Jarausch, *The Enigmatic Chancellor,* **pp. 377–8**

Questions

1 Does **6.16** give a true impression of the Kaiser's influence on policy?
2 How far was Bethmann Hollweg's resignation in 1917 the consequence
   of his own inadequacy [**6.17**]?
3 How much difference did the removal of Bethmann Hollweg make to
   Germany's conduct of the war?

The failure of reform

The last hope of preserving the empire was to transform it into a genuine
parliamentary democracy. For this to happen three changes at least were
vital: the Prussian three class electoral system would have to go; ministers
would have to become answerable to the Reichstag rather than to the emperor; and the emperor's personal control over the armed forces would have
to be ended. By the spring of 1917 Bethmann Hollweg was prepared to go
some way towards making these changes. He was now apparently convinced
of the justice of universal suffrage, and while not ready to accept parliamentarisation of the monarchy accepted the need for some ministers at any rate
to be drawn from the Reichstag. He could see no prospect, however, of
removing the *Kommandogewalt*.

To make such changes required both the approval of the emperor and of
the Reichstag. Wilhelm was induced in his Easter message to the German
people to offer at least the prospect of constitutional reform – but only at the
end of the war. By July Wilhelm was prepared to go further, and to accept
leaders of political parties into the cabinet. But by this stage Bethmann
Hollweg's position was becoming untenable, as we have seen. Attacked on
the left because his projected reforms did not go far enough, and on the right
because they went too far Bethmann Hollweg never secured the whole-
hearted support of the Reichstag and was ousted from office by an unholy
alliance between the duo, Hindenburg and Ludendorff, and the Centre and
National Liberal parties.

His immediate successor, Georg Michaelis, had neither the will nor the opportunity to take up the cause of constitutional reform. He was chancellor for only three months. His replacement in October 1917, Count Georg von Hertling, the former prime minister of Bavaria, was sympathetic to reform of the Prussian electoral system, if not to the parliamentarisation of the monarchy. He too ran into as much opposition as Bethmann Hollweg, as the comments of Colonel Bauer, Ludendorff's aide, indicate only too clearly **[6.19]**. Reform of the empire had to wait until the chancellorship of Maximilian of Baden in October 1918, by which stage it was too late.

6.18   Bethmann Hollweg's proposals, April 1917

I favor the establishment of closer and stronger ties between government and parliament, appropriate to our constitution, with the intent of leading not to formal Reichstag responsibility but to actual participation ... I have become convinced that to avoid great upheavals in the state we can introduce only equal suffrage after the war ... H.M. is still free to grant equal suffrage to the people on   5
his own initiative, and to do so now is my most humble suggestion.

K. H. Jarausch, *The Enigmatic Chancellor,* **p. 344**

6.19   Colonel Bauer's comments on equal suffrage, April 1918

It should be constantly emphasised that equal suffrage means the end for Prussia, as it does for any other state. What is the point of all these sacrifices now, if in the end we are going to suffocate under Jews and proletarians?

H-U. Wehler, *The German Empire,* **p. 237**

Questions

1   Were Bethmann Hollweg's reform proposals in 1917 **[6.18]** anything more than constitutional window–dressing?
2   How far do the views expressed in **6.19** account for the failure of Bethmann Hollweg's reform proposals?

The polarisation of parties

The *Burgfrieden* announced on 4 August 1914 persisted for a remarkably long time, at any rate so far as the major political parties were concerned. A majority of the SPD continued to vote war credits until the summer of 1918.

By 1916, however, serious rifts were beginning to appear. The few isolated voices raised against support of the war, those of Rosa Luxemburg and Karl Liebknecht in particular, emerged as a distinctive group in the spring of 1916; it took its name from the publication of a clandestine newspaper, *Spartakus*, whose first proper issue came out in September of that year. Further to the left of the Spartacists were the International Socialists of Germany, led by a radical journalist called Johann Knieff. Links were established with exiled Bolsheviks such as Karl Radek who contributed to their newspaper, *Arbeiterpolitik*. Radek urged a complete break with the SPD.

Within the official ranks of the SPD there was a growing body of opinion opposed to the war. In December 1915 thirty-eight members of the parliamentary party voted against war credits in a party meeting and, of these, twenty voted publicly against them in the Reichstag. On Mayday 1916 Liebknecht organised a demonstration in Berlin, calling for 'bread, freedom, peace'. He was sentenced to four years' penal servitude.

In January 1917 a joint conference was organised between members of the Social Democratic Working Group, opposed to war credits, and the Spartacists. The official leadership of the SPD claimed that this amounted to 'a separate organisation against the party' and this led to a further conference at Gotha in April 1917 at which the Independent Social Democratic Party (*Unabhängige Sozialdemokratische Partei Deutschlands* – USPD) was created. Delegates from ninety-one constituencies attended the conference, and within a year the party claimed over 100,000 members. Unfortunately, other left-wing groups failed to unite under its umbrella, and the party lacked strong leadership or any specific aims [6.20]. It did, however, have the courage alone of the parties in the Reichstag to vote against the treaty of Brest-Litovsk [6.21].

After the passage of the Peace Resolution in July 1917 there were opposite stirrings on the right, inspired by fears of a compromise peace and political reforms at home. On 3 September 1917 an East Prussian civil servant, Wolfgang Kapp, and Admiral Tirpitz (now retired) joined forces in founding the Fatherland Party (*Vaterlandspartei*). Kapp became its chairman, and Tirpitz its vice-chairman. It put forward a massive programme of annexations and had support from right-wing industrialists and pressure groups such as the Pan-German League. Some idea of its attitudes to war can be gained from **6.22**. By July 1918 it claimed a membership of over 1.25 million, with 2,536 separate branches. The widening of the political spectrum in 1917 and 1918 is reflected in these developments, which are illustrated in **6.20–6.22**.

6.20   Hugo Haase (leader of the USPD) defines the aims of his party at the Gotha Conference, April 1917

In his opening address Haase emphasised that the conference was to open the path to 'a truly socialist policy which is sharply divided from the policy of the government socialists who have made their peace with the bourgeois parties'.

F. L. Carsten, *War against War, British and German Radical Movements in the First World War*, p. 53

6.21   Haase's speech in opposition to the treaty of Brest-Litovsk

Russia is forced to accept a peace of violence at which the imagination boggles. It must cede straight away Courland, Riga, Lithuania, Poland ... The inhabitants of these lands do not want the reactionary Prussian order with which they are to be blessed. They are able to preserve order if not only the Russian, but also the German troops are withdrawn.

F. L. Carsten, *War against War*, p. 194

6.22(a)   Tirpitz's view of the war at the founding of the Fatherland Party, 2 September 1917

The war has developed into a life and death struggle between two world philosophies: the German and the Anglo-American. The question today is whether we can hold our own against Anglo-Americanism or whether we must sink down and become mere manure for others ... The colossal struggle which Germany is now waging is therefore not one for Germany alone; what is really at   5 issue is the liberty of the continent of Europe and its peoples against the all-devouring tyranny of Anglo-Americanism.

F. Fischer, *Germany's Aims in the First World War*, p. 432

6.22(b)   Tirpitz defends the Fatherland Party in his memoirs

At this very time, if it was necessary and possible to conclude a peace of renunciation (which the Fatherland Party could never prevent), the Government, relying on the existence of that party could have stood out for better terms. It is also essential to point out that during the whole period of the party's existence no opportunity arose for a peace of understanding. Nothing but the everlasting and   5 baseless delusion of our democrats, that Germany, to obtain an acceptable peace, had but to ask for it, made it possible to attach the name of 'Prolongers of the war' to the men whose views, had they been allowed to prevail from the first, would have brought the war more rapidly to one or other conclusion. The parties really guilty of prolonging the war are those who steadily undermined our power   10

of resistance, and gave the Entente that certainty to which Lloyd George has
given expression ... If anything can give us hope that German patriotism will
again build us a strong and habitable German home, it is the fact that, after three
years of war, and in spite of the activities of Bethmann and the democrats, a
movement could arise of such power and patriotic feeling as the Fatherland party. |5|

A. von Tirpitz, *My Memoirs*, vol. 2, pp. 334–5

Questions

1   How do you account for the willingness of the SPD to vote for war
    credits until 1918?
2   How far is the weakness of the left in Germany between 1914 and 1918
    to be explained by its internal divisions [**6.20, 6.21**]?
3   In the light of **6.22(a)** examine Tirpitz's claim in **6.22(b)** that it was the
    parties 'who steadily undermined our power of resistance' who were
    'really guilty of prolonging the war'.
4   Explain why the Fatherland party grew so much more rapidly than the
    Independent Socialist party in 1917–18.
5   At what point did the war begin to widen political divisions in Germany
    rather than to narrow them?

The ending of the empire

When it finally came, the end of the empire occurred with astonishing rapidity and in scenes of widespread confusion. On 29 September Ludendorff
coupled his impassioned plea for an armistice with a demand for a 'revolution from above', partly to forestall a revolution from below, partly to saddle
democratically chosen politicians with responsibility for German defeat
[**6.23**]. Under pressure from the military, Hertling resigned the chancellorship which, on October 3, was assumed by Prince Max of Baden, a known
advocate of constitutional reforms and a negotiated peace, despite the fact
that he was also the Kaiser's first cousin. Prince Max got to work rapidly.
On 4 October negotiations were opened with President Wilson. On 5
October Prince Max in his opening speech to the Reichstag promised
ministerial responsibility to the Reichstag, reform of the Prussian electoral
system and an ending to the law of siege which gave control over civilian
governments to the military in time of war.

    The negotiation of armistice terms proved more difficult, both
Hindenburg and Ludendorff seeing them as an opportunity for a breathing

space rather than the prelude to peace. Wilson insisted on immediate abandonment of U-boat warfare, a demand strongly resisted by Hindenburg, and in his third note delivered on 23 October Wilson argued that 'if it [the US government] must deal with the military masters and monarchical autocrats of Germany now ... it must demand, not peace negotiations, but surrender'.

This note provoked a furious protest from the German High Command. A draft proclamation, to which Ludendorff gave his signature, fell into the hands of a soldier telegraphist who despatched it to the Independent Socialist Headquarters in Berlin [6.24]. When released in the Reichstag it caused an immediate outcry, and led Prince Max to insist on Ludendorff's resignation as the price of his own continuation in office. On 26 October Ludendorff finally resigned, though Hindenburg stayed on. **6.23** and **6.24** illustrate these events.

6.23(a)   Admiral Paul von Hintze, foreign secretary at the time, describes the proceedings at Spa on 29 September 1918

General Ludendorff explained the military situation ... the condition of the army required immediate ceasefire in order to avert a catastrophe ...
As a way out of this situation I expounded: Gathering together *all* the nation's forces for defence in the final struggle.
  As means I mentioned: 1. Dictatorship; the dictatorship would be tied to the   5
condition that military successes, if not victory, could be promised in the foreseeable future, otherwise it would be followed by revolution or chaos.
2. Revolution from above; the sudden swing from confidence in victory to defeat must deal a blow to the nation, the consequences of which Empire and dynasty would hardly survive. To anticipate the shock unleash a people's war, which   10
would send the last man to the front – let the broadest circles be given an interest in the outcome by drawing them into government.
3. To procure the immediate ceasefire, which the OHL demanded: an invitation to conclude peace *via* the President of the United States, on the basis of published proposals.   15
  General Ludendorff rejected dictatorship: Victory would be impossible, the state of the army demanded rather immediate ceasefire. The Field Marshal [Hindenburg] and General Ludendorff approved the revolution from above.

I. Porter and I. D. Amour, *Imperial Germany*, pp. 105–6

6.23(b)   Ludendorff explains the political situation to his subordinates at OHL, 1 October 1918, as recorded by Colonel von Thaer, an eyewitness

Excellency Ludendorff added: 'At the moment we do not have a chancellor. Who it will be is unclear. *But I have asked H.M. to bring those circles into the government now, who we have primarily to thank that we have got to this stage.* So

we are going to let these men move into the ministries. They are going to have to conclude the peace that has to be concluded. They are going to have to eat the   5
soup they have cooked for us!'

I. Porter and I. D. Armour, *Imperial Germany*, pp. 106–7

6.24   Ludendorff's draft proclamation, 24 October 1918

Wilson's answer is a demand for unconditional surrender. It is thus unacceptable to us soldiers. It proves that our enemy's desire for our destruction, which let loose the war of 1914, still exists undiminished. It proves, further, that our enemies use the phrase 'a just peace' merely to deceive us and break our resistance. Wilson's answer can thus be nothing for us soldiers but a challenge to   5
continue our resistance with all our strength.

R. B. Asprey, *The German High Command*, p. 482

Questions

1   Which of Hintze's proposals on 29 September 1918 [**6.23(a)**] did Ludendorff accept?
2   Comment with reference to **6.23(a)** on Ludendorff's gibe in **6.23(b)** 'They are going to have to eat the soup they have cooked for us!'
3   What evidence can you cite to refute Ludendorff's arguments in **6.24**?

 Even at this stage there were those who believed that all was not lost, or at any rate that Germany should go down fighting. On 28 October the German battlefleet was ordered to raise steam in preparation for a final sortie into the North Sea. On 29 October several ships' crews refused to weigh anchor for such a desperate enterprise and by 3 November a full-scale mutiny had broken out and Kiel was controlled by the sailors of the fleet. Between 6 and 9 November there were sympathetic workers' demonstrations in cities as far apart as Bremen, Cologne and Munich. Karl Liebknecht, who had been released on 23 October, was planning a rising in Berlin for 8 November. It became increasingly clear to Prince Max and the Majority Socialists that if they were to avert a full-blown revolution the Kaiser would have to go.

 On 6 November, General Groener, who had replaced Ludendorff on 26 October, was summoned to Berlin where he met Ebert, leader of the Majority Socialists. He was told that unless the Kaiser abdicated the government would no longer be able to control the workers. The Kaiser, unfortunately, had left Berlin for army headquarters at Spa and could only be reached by telephone. On 8 November Prince Max urged his cousin to abdicate: 'Your abdication has become necessary to save Germany from civil war'. The Kaiser flatly refused. On the following day the Majority Socialists withdrew their support from the government and at 11.30 a.m. Prince Max decided to act on his own initiative. He released to the press a draft announcement of Wilhelm's abdication [6.25]. At about the same time, Groener had an audience with Wilhelm at Spa, at which he told the Kaiser that he could no longer rely on the support of the army [6.26]. Wilhelm still refused to accept his position, and when news of Prince Max's announcement came through at about 1.30 p.m. he exclaimed 'Treason, gentlemen, barefaced treason!' By five o'clock that afternoon he had accepted his fate. On the following morning, 10 November, he left for Holland where he would spend the rest of his life in exile. At 11.00 a.m. on 11 November the armistice was signed. The Second Reich ended, as it began, on the battlefield.

6.25   The announcement of Wilhelm's abdication, 9 November 1918

The Emperor and King has decided to renounce the throne. The Imperial Chancellor will remain in office until the questions connected with the abdication of the Emperor, the renunciation of the throne of Germany and of Prussia by the Crown Prince, and the setting up of a regency have been settled.

R. M. Watt, *The Kings Depart*, **p. 218**

6.26   General Groener indicates the attitude of the army to the Kaiser, 9 November 1918

The army will march home in peace and order under its leaders and commanding generals, but not under the command of Your Majesty, for it no longer stands behind Your Majesty.

A. Palmer, *The Kaiser, Warlord of the Second Reich*, **p. 210**

Questions

1   When and why did the Kaiser's abdication become inevitable [6.25, 6.26]?
2   Examine the view that it was only the strains imposed by the First World War that made the Second Reich unworkable.

Bibliography

Bibliographical

Tracey J. Kay, Bibliographical essay in *Modern Germany Reconsidered*, ed. G. Martel, London, 1992 (Routledge)
I. Porter and I. D. Armour, *Imperial Germany 1890–1918*, London, 1991 (Longman)

Original Sources

F. von Bernhardi, *Germany and the Next War*, London, 1914 (Arnold)
A. J. Butler (ed.), *Otto von Bismarck, the Man and Statesman, being the Reflections and Reminiscences of Otto, Prince von Bismarck*, London, 1898 (Smith, Elder and Co.)
I. Geiss (ed.), *July 1914: The Outbreak of the First World War: Selected Documents*, London, 1967 (Batsford)
Fragen an die deutsche Geschichte, Bonn, 1981 (Deutscher Bundestag)
T. S. Hamerow (ed.), *The Age of Bismarck, Documents and Interpretation*, New York, 1973 (Harper and Row)
W. N. Medlicott and D. K. Coveney (eds.), *Bismarck and Europe*, London, 1971 (Arnold)
N. Rich and M. H. Fisher (eds.), *The Holstein Papers*, Cambridge, 1955 (Cambridge University Press)
J. C. G. Röhl, *From Bismarck to Hitler, The Problem of Continuity in German History*, London, 1971 (Longman)
H. Rothfels, *Bismarck und der Staat*, Stuttgart, 1958 (Kohlhammer)
W. M. Simon (ed.), *Germany in the Age of Bismarck*, London, 1974 (Allen and Unwin)
L. L. Snyder (ed.), *Documents of German History*, Rutgers, 1958 (Rutgers University Press)
Alfred von Tirpitz, *My Memoirs*, London, 1919 (Hurst and Blackett)

General Background

V. R. Berghahn, *Modern Germany, Society, Economy and Politics in the Twentieth Century*, Cambridge, 1982 (Cambridge University Press)
D. Blackbourn and G. Eley, *The Peculiarities of German History*, Oxford, 1984 (Oxford University Press)
G. A. Craig, *Germany, 1866–1945*, Oxford, 1978 (Oxford University Press)
G. Martel (ed.) *Modern Germany Reconsidered*, London, 1992 (Routledge)

A. J. P. Taylor, *The Struggle for Mastery in Europe*, Oxford, 1954 (Oxford University Press)
H-U. Wehler, *The German Empire, 1871–1918*, Leamington Spa, 1985 (Berg Publishers)

Germany 1871–1890

L. Gall, *Bismarck, the White Revolutionary*, vol. 2, London, 1982 (Unwin Hyman Ltd)
C. Grant Robertson, *Bismarck*, London, 1918 (Constable)
B. and M. Pawley, *Rome and Canterbury through the Centuries*, London, 1974 (Mowbrays)
F. Stern, *Gold and Iron: Bismarck, Bleichröder and the Building of the German Empire*, London, 1987 (Penguin Books)
A. J. P. Taylor, *Bismarck, the Man and the Statesman*, London, 1955 (Hamish Hamilton)

Germany, 1890–1914

L. Cecil, *Wilhelm II, Prince and Emperor*, Chapel Hill, 1989 (University of North Carolina Press)
K. A. Lerman, *The Chancellor as Courtier: Bernhard von Bülow and the Governance of Germany*, Cambridge, 1990 (Cambridge University Press)
K. H. Jarausch, *The Enigmatic Chancellor: Bethmann Hollweg and the Hubris of Imperial Germany*, London, 1973 (Yale University Press)
A. Palmer, *The Kaiser, Warlord of the Second Reich*, London, 1978 (Weidenfeld and Nicolson)
J. C. G. Röhl, *Germany without Bismarck: the Crisis of Government in the Second Reich*, London, 1967 (Batsford)
J. C. G. Röhl and N. Sombart (eds.), *Kaiser Wilhelm II, New Interpretations*, Cambridge, 1982 (Cambridge University Press)

Foreign Policy

V. R. Berghahn, *Germany and the Approach of War*, London, 1993 (Macmillan)
R. J. W. Evans and H. P. von Strandmann (eds.), *The Causes of the First World War*, Oxford, 1988 (Oxford University Press)
F. Fischer, *Germany's Aims in the First World War*, London, 1967 (Chatto and Windus)
F. Fischer, *War of Illusions: German Policy from 1911 to 1914*, London, 1975 (Chatto and Windus)
R. Henig, *The Origins of the First World War*, London, 1989 (Routledge)
J. Joll, *The Origins of the first World War*, London, 1984 (Longman)
P. M. Kennedy, *The Rise of Anglo-German Antagonism, 1860–1914*, London, 1980 (Allen and Unwin)
D. C. B. Lieven, *Russia and the Origins of the First World War*, London, 1983 (Macmillan)J. C. G. Röhl (ed.) *1914: Delusion or Design?*, London, 1973 (Elek)

J. C. G. Röhl (ed) *1914: Delusion or Design?*, London, 1973 (Elek)

Z. Steiner, *Britain and the Origins of the First World War*, London, 1977 (Macmillan)

Germany and the First World War

R. B. Asprey, *The German High Command at War, Hindenburg and Ludendorff and the First World War*, London, 1993 (Little, Brown and Co.)

C. Barnett, *The Swordbearers*, London, 1963 (Eyre and Spottiswoode)

F. L. Carsten, *War against War: British and German Radical Movements in the First World War*, London, 1982 (Batsford)

M. Kitchen, *The Silent Dictatorship: The Politics of the German High Command under Hindenburg and Ludendorff 1916–18*, London, 1976 (Croom Helm)

A. J. Marder, *From the Dreadnought to Scapa Flo*, Oxford, 1978 (Oxford University Press)

R. Pipes, *The Russian Revolution*, London, 1990 (Fontana)

R. M. Watt, *The Kings Depart*, London, 1969 (Pelican Books)

J. W. Wheeler-Bennett, *The Forgotten Peace: Brest-Litovsk, March 1918*, London, 1956 (Macmillan)

Articles

R. J. Evans, 'Kaiser Wilhelm II and German history', *History Review*, No. 11, p. 36

C. Hellawell, 'Reichstag and Repression Imperial Germany 1890–1914', *Modern History Review*, vol. 5, No. 1, p. 26

K. A. Lerman, 'Kaiser Wilhelm II, Last Emperor of Germany', *Modern History Review*, vol 1, No. 2, p. 2

W. Mommsen, 'Domestic factors in German foreign policy before 1914', *Central European History*, 6 (March, 1973), p. 11

J. C. G. Röhl, 'Imperial Germany, The Riddle of 1914, part 1', *Modern History Review*, vol. 2, No. 1, p. 8

J. C. G. Röhl, 'Imperial Germany, The Riddle of 1914, part 2', *Modern History Review*, vol. 2, No. 1, p. 10

B. Waller, 'The Enigma of Bismarck as Chancellor', *Modern History Review*, vol. 2, No. 3, p. 16

Index